ALCHEMY
OF THE GODS

Alchemy of The Gods
By Michael Feeley

Published 2019 by Sazmick Books
Web: www.sazmickbooks.com
Web: www.michael-feeley.com

British Library Cataloguing-in Publication Data.
A catalogue record for this book is available from the British Library.

ISBN: 978-1-912400-05-8 (Paperback)
ISBN: 978-1-912400-39-3 (Ebook)

Printed and bound in the UK using sustainable resources.

ALCHEMY
OF THE GODS

MICHAEL FEELEY

SAZMICK
BOOKS

WHAT OTHERS ARE SAYING ABOUT MICHAEL'S WORK

"Thanks to people like you, we are all moving forward"

"Absolutely mind blowing! Thank you so much for such amazing puzzle solving👌"

"Your knowledge and the way you deliver it is second to none"

"Michael is a fantastic encyclopaedia of knowledge, love his work"

"Brilliant Michael! Absolutely captivating at the highest degree"

"Thank you Mick, you have been and continue to be a great teacher🙏"

"Your insights as well as investigative studies are at the absolute pinnacle of decoding"

"Talk about 'a divine messenger'. You come to mind"!

"You're a conduit for this knowledge. I can't thank you enough for sharing it"

"Fascinating stuff Michael, truly genius"

"The enormous privilege of coming across someone like Michael Feeley has lent sparkling excitement to my quest, as you can feel the energy of his knowledge, his explorations, and his discernment about the discoveries he has made and the huge wealth of understanding that he is so courageously sharing with the rest of us."

"Thanks for the brilliant chat yesterday, actually it was a tutorial for me, as listening to you speak on the topics we explored was inspiring and encouraging. I think that, due to your benevolence and willingness to share, we are all benefitting from your experiences and the years of research and study that you have invested in this work."

"Michael, you kindly gave well over and above the agreed time limit for the call and I received far more than I was scheduled to; thanks for being so dedicated to helping me understand and ensuring that I had ample opportunity to ask any questions I needed to. You answered everything I enquired about with clarity, depth and breadth of knowledge and, what stands out for me is the way you listened intently to everything I said, explaining in detail and giving me a rich learning experience than I will savour. I have followed your work with enthusiasm for a long time and have directed many others to experience the treasure trove of your esoteric knowledge and wisdom. It is such a pleasure to have had this chance to talk with you and I look forward to speaking with you again in the future."

"Michael holds a profound understanding of the ancient knowledge and its history. I am grateful for Michael's generosity in sharing his insight and clear guidance through our skype conversation. My questions were answered and it helps me to take the next step in this journey. Great work Michael. Thank you!"

ACKNOWLEDGEMENTS

I would like to give thanks to my wife, Sarah, for her contributions to this book, namely its design and publication under Sazmick Books Publishing. I would also like to give mention to the beautiful G, and to my family. Thank you to Laura Plumb Sayers, co-organiser of the Probe conference in Blackpool, UK, for being the facilitator of some of my channelled messages and to Sam Wright, also of Probe for giving me a platform to share this wonderful information. I have enjoyed speaking at your conferences, you are all wonderful people.

I would also like to thank renowned international speaker and researcher Mary Rodwell for her foreword. And a big thanks to you for reading the book.

CONTENTS

Introduction:

FOREWORD

By Mary Rodwell - Principal of ACERN and Co-founder FREE

It is with great pleasure to write this foreword for Michael Feeley's book, *Alchemy of the Gods*. I found the information both comprehensive and multidisciplinary. It embodies compelling investigative research into the complexity of human origins. Michael assists the reader to explore new concepts to understand what has been previously interpreted as mysterious, the hidden in terms of human origins and who and what we are. Michael's approach assists the reader to 'connect the dots' as he deciphers new meaning to codes, ancient artefacts and symbology which in combination offer the reader an alternate and multidimensional history of humanity.

Michael's book highlights the 'anomalies' found in human DNA, which indicate Homo Sapiens Sapiens are an intelligently designed species. The 'intelligences' who created our species, are the so called 'gods' that have visited humanity for millennia. These 'gods' added their DNA, creating the hybrid species known as Homo Sapiens Sapiens.

Whistleblower geneticist and renowned Molecular Biologist and co-founder of the DNA molecule Dr Francis Crick states:

"The DNA molecule is the most efficient storage system in the entire Universe. The immensity of complex coded and precise sequenced information is absolutely staggering. The DNA evidence speaks

of intelligent, information baring design. "They" extraterrestrials programmed the molecules so they could therefore teach us about ourselves and how to progress. For life to form by chance is mathematically virtually impossible."

Ref: Ann Krielkamp Francis Crick on DNA: Intelligent Design Exopermaculture, April 14th 2011. http://wwwexopermaculture.com/2011/04/14/francis-crick-on-dna-intelligent-design/

Michael references how the nature of human DNA is so significant to our understanding of who and what we are as a species and the amazing potentials locked within it. DNA that was considered dormant, known as junk DNA, he believes is not junk at all, but when activated holds the key to awakening humanity to its full potential.

Astrophysicist Dr Rudy Schild, co-founder of The Dr Edgar Mitchell Foundation for Research into Extraterrestrial and Extra-ordinary Experiences (FREE) confirms this understanding, and hypothesizes there is far more to human DNA than its physical properties stated:

"I have long understood that the DNA does more than chemistry, and is in resonance with the quantum hologram to bring emotional and spiritual content into our being. The mathematics of how this works in human consciousness involves the soul and has been described to me "with hints of mathematics."

Ref: *Beyond UFO's The Science of Consciousness and Contact with Non-Human Intelligence Vol I* chapter 8, page 496.

The nature of Michael's research combines information that is encoded so that the knowledge is only available to a select few; an 'elite' who deem themselves superior to the rest of humanity due to their genetic family linage. This knowledge is hidden in symbology and encrypted so only this select few can understand what it means. This knowledge allows this 'elite' to retain their power base and control the rest of humanity. Particularly the knowledge of our genetic origins and humanity's hidden potentials.

Michael's investigative expertise, effectively honed by his police training has enabled him to delve into significant and compelling data to assist the 'seeker' to understand the numerous and complex 'clues' left by our ancestors. *Alchemy of the Gods* weaves a tapestry of metaphysical information gleaned from ancient artefacts, scripts, codes and symbology to indicate a far more complex understanding of human origins than we have been led to believe. It's extraordinary information and may challenge some readers but Michael offers compelling evidence to explain its validity.

Michael expertly leads the reader through this secret esoteric matrix and how we can decode and interpret this information, the knowledge we can all access to become an empowered multidimensionally aware human. It gives the understanding that we can transcend our limited and limiting programming. Programming which has been directed and endorsed by this 'elite' group who wish to keep humanity enslaved. *Alchemy of the Gods* is a fascinating journey exploring numerology, ancient religious texts, symbology, anthropology, archeology, biology and more. Michael's research offers a broader template to understanding humanity's hidden past that has kept us from the awareness of who we are.

Alchemy of the Gods includes Michael's personal story, which is pivotal I believe, as he courageously shares how his own multidimensional experiences with non-human intelligences (NHI) have been significant to his motivation to actively seek out truth. One of the significant patterns with encounter experiences is that the individuals may become passionate, almost obsessed to discover the truth of who and what they are. I believe Michael's interactions with these 'intelligences' may well have been a guiding factor in his quest to uncover the understanding of such mysteries. It is certainly true of those that have encounters with Unidentified Ariel Phenomenon (UAP). These 'sightings' may well include an encounter not recalled consciously but accompanied by 'downloads' of information. Certainly, this information demonstrates we need to expand our understanding of who and what we think we are to explore our hidden potential. Michael's research indicates that 'We are the Gods'. *Alchemy of the Gods* offers the reader a fascinating journey through the matrix. A must read for those seeking to know who or what we are.

Mary Rodwell

- author *Awakening* (2002) & *The New Human* (2016), Principal of *Australian Close Encounter Resource Network* www.acern.com.au. Co-founder *The Dr Edgar Mitchell Foundation for Extraterrestrial and Extraordinary Experiences* (FREE) www.Experiencer.org

References

Rodwell, Mary. *AWAKENING, How Extraterrestrial Contact Can Transform your life* (2002) revised (2010.) New Mind Publishers

Rodwell, Mary. *THE NEW HUMAN, Awakening to Our Cosmic Heritage.* New Mind Publishers (2016)

Beyond UFO's Vol 1 Editors Re Hernandez JD, MCP. Dr Jon Klimo PhD Dr Rudy Schild PhD www.Experiencer.org published 2018

AUSTRALIAN CLOSE ENCOUNTER RESEARCH NETWORK

ABOUT THE AUTHOR

Michael Feeley was born of humble beginnings, the son of a working father and a full-time mother in the West Midlands, within the industrial heartland of England and a descendent of Irish Celtic Kings through his father's side. In a time of no computers, no iPods or mobile phones, and only three channels on TV, it was the dark ages to the youth of today. This is hard to imagine in the modern era of instant global digital fingertip access and technology galore.

From a very early age, between the age of 6 and 7, Michael began to have adult conversations with himself, questioning reality and questioning what we were being told to believe by the likes of school teachers and movie producers, amongst other mediums. He would sit through movies such as 'The 10 Commandments' with Charlton Heston, and seriously contemplate if these miracles really happened or if they were just a story. He was a quiet child who preferred the solitude of his bedroom that gave him a comfort of anti-limelight shadows.

Having eventually achieved Ordinary Level (0 Level) qualifications at state secondary school, Michael held down numerous jobs before finally achieving his ambition of becoming a police officer, which he did for 17 years in England's two largest cities, London and Birmingham. Eighteen weeks of gruelling exams, morning uniform inspections, tested scenarios, and continuous other tests assessed his general ability for the role. A high failure rate was the norm, in fact, a 35% failure rate, but Michael was determined not to be that statistic. A doctor and several nurses were permanently on-site for the stress factor and general push and pull on the body as the weeks took their toll. With each week the horizon drew closer, and that light at the end of the tunnel came forever nearer to the passing out parade that would see Michael leave the training environment and venture onto the mean streets to start his new career. Eighteen exams later, eighteen weeks of shouting and screaming at the hands of the ex-army drill instructors, and eighteen weeks of torrential tests had now come to a delightful end.

During those 17 years, Michael achieved many accolades and awards including commendations for bravery, and was a high-performing, well-respected, and reliable officer, sought after by many departments within the police service. He was considered an expert eye witness in any UK courtroom. He was a trained investigator and solved many crimes of differing magnitudes.

If he had retrospect in a bottle, then things may have been different from the onset, he may never have joined the police force had he have known that he would be leaving in 2009. Michael had never anticipated leaving and he thought that he was going to be there forever and a day and then some more. The police was his first marriage, and those who get married don't often contemplate divorce, but it can, in certain circumstances, just happen. Sometimes, life has different plans and life directs you to where you need to be at that time, often for a greater purpose than we can possibly know at the time. Sometimes, we find ourselves unknowingly stepping from each stepping stone, venturing in a direction we cannot immediately see. As Michael was subsequently told in a galactic channelled message *"You do not like injustice especially to those who cannot defend themselves. This is why you left the work you did as you could see this every day around you. Your energies did not allow you to stay in this environment"*

The lesson that it taught Michael and the experience that it gave him has now come into fruition with his new path of ancient investigations. It was during his time as a police officer that he met his wife, Sarah, and their relationship blossomed during inner city riots and many long hours within police vehicles spanning from early morning to another early morning without a gap in-between. Michael and Sarah were Sardines in a police tin to a married couple in a relatively short period of time.

In 2009, his life was to change and cause him to leave his first marriage, the police service. No-one usually leaves the police, they retire from it after 30 plus years.

Not only was he witnessing corruption and the deliberate fabrication of 'Home Office' figures (the Home Office is the UK Government's Department for Prisons and Police/Immigration, et al.), he was also experiencing many events in his personal life that can only be described as supernatural and paranormal, which he talks about in his earlier books and touches upon in this one.

Michael's police career, although ending abruptly, taught him the skill of evidence gathering and investigation. As a result, Michael can now piece codes and metaphors together, along with hidden encrypted messages that most people cannot see. He was shown a golden key in his mind's eye, which symbolises locked knowledge and closely guarded secrets that he now reveals.

The skill of the investigator is to make connections, and Michael has made an ancient connection that has formed a blueprint for the whole ancient world, proving that they had access to the same knowledge base and were therefore connected to one another, something that he documented in his book, 'The Ancient Code – A Serpent Fire'. A lot of Michael's information comes to him by what is known as 'Hyper-Communication', which arrives in the form of inspiration or intuition. This is where you access information outside of your normal scope and knowledge base.

In this book, Michael concentrates on the world of ancient mysteries and humanity as a higher type of human and how those who understood the true mysteries reached the 'philosopher's stone', the wisdom stone, or stone of wisdom. Due to Michael's in-depth work, he has been approached by various illuminati (enlightened ones) groups who have attempted to recruit him into their ranks. He has also been privately told that the information that he is revealing would take an initiate many years to discover and learn, with comments about its accuracy. He has always declined their offers to join, despite the numerous promises of personal gain.

Michael now writes numerous books and e-books, contributes regularly to global radio shows and various magazines, has guest featured on independent documentaries such as 'Strawman – The Nature of the Cage', and is also a public conference speaker, travelling around the UK to give presentations which has now extended beyond the UK to America with a conference talk in San Francisco in February 2020. He is an esoteric journalist who uncovers many of the world's greatest mysteries and shows a connection between them, something rarely seen. Two of Michael's books - *The Ancient Code – A Serpent Fire* and *The Annunaki Of Nibiru and the Snakemen Of Eridu* - have both recently been featured in the August-September 2019 edition of *Nexus Magazine*.

Michael is about to reveal to you a greater reality about humanity and its place in the cosmos.

"At times you wonder how you get the information you do. Well my dear friend we channel this to you. Although you may not look on yourself as a medium, without these mediumistic abilities, you would not be able to hear us and do your work" (Galactic channelled message to Michael.)

'Alchemy of the Gods'...

ABOUT THE BOOK

So what is the purpose of this book? The purpose of this book is to show you that each and every ancient culture operated from the same deeper knowledge base and had connections to not only each other, but also to other worlds. It will show you that they created a higher type of human through the likes of alchemy and sound. Even when you see a church or other religious building, they display a beautiful geometry. This geometry was not just put there because it looks good, but because it creates a resonance structure that has a wavelength of pure consciousness and a *Tri-Thalamic Entrainment Frequency*. This frequency takes you to a vibration of sanctity. Even within ancient monasteries, monks used their voice harmonies to re-create the Solfeggio scale, which was an ancient monastery tone that imparted spiritual blessings.

These are the Solfeggio frequencies:

UT – 396 Hz – transforms grief into joy and guilt into forgiveness

RE – 417 Hz – clears negativity and removes subconscious blockages

MI – 528 Hz – stimulates love, restores equilibrium, repairs DNA

FA – 639 Hz – strengthens relationships, family, and community unity

SOL – 741 Hz – physically cleanses the body from all types of toxins

LA – 852 Hz – awakens intuition and helps you return to spiritual balance

These frequencies opened up their inner portals of wisdom

through the pineal gland, which is a route to enlightenment. They were the masters of frequency and sound, something I have personally witnessed at Stonehenge.

But this knowledge has been encrypted in such likes as the story of Christ and the gigantic monoliths and monuments such as the pyramids of the world - and not only this world - that have all stood the test of time. The book will also make mention of the fact that those with this esoteric gnosis considered themselves walking Gods. They had a higher consciousness, which means a mystical awareness. These Gods are often depicted as giants for metaphorical reasons.

(Giant – Metaphor for a Higher Than Average Insight)

This book tells you how to achieve and attain Godhood, the ancient way. I will take you to your own Machu Picchu, which means Old Mountain, and a mountain is symbolic of a higher connection or a place of revelation. Machu Picchu was, in effect, an ancient ascension school, the classroom of which was high in the mountains, a place closer to God. This is the same meaning of pyramid steps that lead closer to God.

I will show you how the Giza pyramids are a giant replica of the third eye of spiritual sight, that their subterranean chambers represent the sub-conscious mind, how the civilisation that was ancient Egypt had a principle of consciousness and spiritual awareness, and that it is a culture that still lives on within the world's secret societies today. Egypt was the origin of alchemy, formerly known as khem, and alchemy means 'the chemistry of God'. This alchemy runs all the way through the very fabric of the world's religions and Christianity. I will show you how the heads of Easter Island represent the divine mind, how Stonehenge is a large enigma machine to decipher messages within sound waves, and how Silbury Hill in Avebury is a portal to planet Mars. I will show you that crop circles, Egyptian hieroglyphs, and the Nazca Lines contain within them sound wave messages shown to us in an ideogram and ideograph format with the use of diatonic ratios.

I will show you how famous biblical icons and characters such as Jesus Christ, Mary Magdalene, Moses, Noah, Mary and Joseph, Adam and Eve, and many others are simply a metaphor for this deeper knowledge of self and were not actual people, a fact that the high priests fully know. Our most loved biblical stories are not real, but instead are a hidden message.

I will show you how the famous Annunaki story of the ancient Sumerian scrolls was wrongly deciphered by renowned author Zecharia Sitchin and that they are really telling us of our genetic higher human potential through the metaphors that have become their Gods, such as Anu, Enki, and Enlil and Alalu. This is not a popular stance amongst the UFO community.

The book will show how human DNA is not from Earth and that human languages are a reflection of that inherent DNA, not random. If our physicality is the product of Orion and our DNA is not from Earth, then that can only leave one conclusion, we are not from here and, as I say later in the book, the Annunaki story is therefore misinterpreted at its most major point, bringing it all into question. It will show how different looking humans occur as a result of how genetics work, which are determined by how genes cross one another, which has relevance to planet X of the Annunaki story. The book will also show you that there is a section of the population that know the ancient secrets and that they have kept it secret from the masses. I will now introduce you to some of those knowledge keepers.

AN INTRODUCTION TO THOSE BEHIND THE MASK

The hidden secret of many Mystery Schools - whether that is Egypt, Gnostics, Kabballah, or even the Alchemists - is the transmutation of self into a higher type of human. It is also the basis of every ancient culture I have researched. A major part of that transmutation process is sacred sexuality and the balance of opposites, not just balance, but the complete merging into non-duality. This sacred sexuality can be seen throughout the ancient world, the mysteries, and even the Bible and other religious scriptures. This merging of sexuality gives us the Star of David, both the upright and inverted triangle combined. But we need to control the fish of sea which is our semen/sperm, the sea of men (semen), which is code for the control of our sexual urges and sexual energy. It is the mystery fertility philosophy. The mushroom is another symbol hidden within the Church, as the mushroom is the symbol of the phallic, and therefore male, fertility, which I will come back to later.

(Masculine And Feminine Sexuality Gives Us The Star Of David)

At this point, I am going to briefly introduce you to just some of the groups who will form part of this book, the groups who hold onto this sacred esoteric knowledge of self. Not all of them act out of malice and intention of concealing the truth - some were driven underground - but, nevertheless, there is an effort to keep the truth away from the population by whatever means. I do not align to, or advocate, any of them, but their knowledge bases are at the deepest levels of esoteric knowledge.

Gnostics:

Gnosticism (from Ancient Greek: γνωστικός gnostikos, *having knowledge*, from γνῶσις gnōsis) knowledge is a modern name for a variety of ancient religious ideas and systems, originating in Jewish Christian milieux in the first and second century AD. These systems believed that the material world is created by an emanation, or 'works', of a lower god (demiurge), trapping the divine spark within the human body. This divine spark could be liberated by gnosis: spiritual knowledge acquired through direct experience. The serpent God of the Gnostics is Serapis, which is

Osiris-Apis of Ancient Egypt, which became Serapis. We could then go into the ascended masters of the New Age (New Cage) with Serapis Bey of Egypt. 'Bey' means 'the realm of Bey' which, in its original context, means 'a divine being'. It also leads us onto the worship of the sacred bull, which I also mention later in the book.

Kabbalah:

Kabbalah (Hebrew: הַקַבָּלַה, literally "reception, tradition" or "correspondence") is an esoteric method, discipline, and school of thought of Judaism. A traditional Kabbalist in Judaism is called a Mequbbāl (לְבָוּקְמ). The definition of Kabbalah varies according to the tradition and aims of those following it, from its religious origin as an integral part of Judaism to its later adaptations in Western esotericism (Christian Kabbalah and Hermetic Qabalah). Jewish Kabbalah is a set of esoteric teachings meant to explain the relationship between God, the unchanging, eternal, and mysterious Ein Sof (אֵין סוֹף, "The Infinite"), and the mortal and finite universe (God's creation). It forms the foundation of mystical religious interpretations within Judaism. The likes of the Pharisees, meaning 'to separate' or 'detach', form part of the Kabballah, and they also wrote the Dead Sea Scrolls. The Kabballah also gives rise to Masonry and, as Rabbi Isaac Wise said, "*Freemasonry is a Jewish establishment*". Masonry is also relevant in some sections of this book.

Within the Kabbalah, you also have several branches:

The Christian Kabballah, who were Jews who converted to the Roman Catholic Church in Spain, created the holy office of the Inquisition, which was Judaism in secrecy. This resulted in the extinction of many who were deemed heretics. 'Heretic' means 'to choose', and if you didn't choose the doctrine of the Church, you were killed. Even in the modern day, with The London Eye, we see reference to this. The London Eye represents the Catherine wheel of torture which has 32 pods, representing the 32 paths of wisdom within the 33 degrees. The London Eye is the masonic compass marking the solstice and the 23 degrees of Earth's tilt, and the dot within the circle is the Monad. The Monad, in early Christian Gnostic writings, is an adaptation of concepts of the Monad in Greek philosophy to Christian Gnostic belief systems of one unit, oneness.

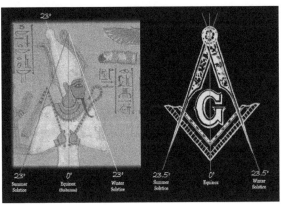

(Above - London Eye, Below - The Monad)

The Hermetic Kaballah is for certain individuals with specialised knowledge who could understand its concepts.

"He who does not seek it is not likely to find it" – Paracelsus

Numerology is important to the Kabbalah, such as the number 22 since the Hebrew alphabet has 22 vibrational letters. It is also why tragic events, which are not what they are always reported to be, contain a numerical fingerprint. This power number is an important number to the likes of Freemasons and Gnostics, as it is the number of the 'Sons of Light', which derives from the 22 bones of the human skull and is where we get the light to become enlightened. The human skull is also Golgotha, the place of skulls. It is also the deeper meaning of the Skull & Crossbones logo of the secret society of the same name, with the addition of number 3 which, in the Hebrew Kabbalah, is the 'Binah', meaning 'understanding', another reference to consciousness. This gives us the skull and crossbones logo 322. The number 22 is on the third octave which also then gves us 322 vibrationally. The word Illuminati, which means 'enlightened ones', the rulers of Earth, equals 120 as so, I=9, L=12,L=12,U=21,M=13,I=9,N=14,A=1,T=20 ,I=9. 120 means divine time in waiting. 120 also has the essence of the number 3, as such, 1+2+0=3. 3 is Binah which is understanding.

22 is also the symbol of the original Christian cross - the Tau cross - which means 'the end' or the furthest development in the material realm.

Not only does this number mean 'enlightenment', but it is also used by certain secret groups as a hidden fingerprint at the scene of various events. For example, the 2017 concert of Ariana Grande in Manchester, where the bomb of a suicide bomber exploded and killed 22 people!

So, let's see how this number contributed to this tragic event in addition to 22 fatalities.

The explosion occurred on 22nd May after the last song. Song 22 had been played in a playlist set containing 22 songs. This song was number 1 in the charts for 22 weeks. The suicide bomber, Salman Abedi, was 22 years of age.

The bomb exploded at 22:30, and even that contains the number 22.

You can form your own opinions as to whether or not this is mathematically possible to be a coincidence.

In the Bible, which is a division of the Hebrew Scriptures (Script), numbers feature repeatedly, not for numbers sake but because specific numbers or number sequences have an esoteric meaning to the secret brotherhoods.

Even the number 8 has a Hebrew name of Shemanah, which has a value of 401. 401 is the value of the name Isaiah. I will go more into the number 8 with Christ in the garden of Gethsemane later.

The number 22 is the Bible wheel with its 22 spokes, and the number 22 unites the whole scriptures of the Bible itself. And this Bible wheel with its 22 spokes is numerically important. The Hebrew alphabet has 22 letters, which is a vibrational text.

We have such celebrations as Pentecost, or Pentecostal, which means 50, celebrated on the 50th day of the week of weeks. Pentecost (50) is on the seventh octave. On spoke 8 of this Bible wheel, we find the book of Ruth.

So we have the number 8 which is on the first octave, the number 22 on the third octave, and the number 50 (Pentecost) on the seventh octave, and this is also why the British monetary coin -

the 50 pence piece - has seven sides. This gives us an esoteric code of 137. 137 is the numerical value of the word Kabbalah. It is also the 33rd prime number and 33 is relevant to Christ, as you will later see. The number 137 is the connection between the unseen and seen force, the number which is the interaction between the vessel and light and is how the vessel absorbs light. Only by way of consciousness can we absorb and connect to light.

137 is also an important Zohar number, and 'Zohar' means 'radiance' (light). It is the chief text of the Kabbalah, presented as an allegorical or mystical interpretation of the Pentateuch (5 books, there are 5 books in the Torah). The number 5 is the number of the Pentagram and 'realised man', hence the 5 wounds of Christ!

1+3+7 = 11, which is also an important Kabbalah number; there are 304:805 letters in the Torah and, if we reverse the numbers in pairs, we get 50+84+03 = 137.

Torah means 'the mark' (hit the mark), in other words the 'bullseye', which is the pineal gland - esoterically this is enlightened consciousness.

Hebrew letters are also numbers and each letter starts with a dot. The dot means universal consciousness, and the key to all knowledge is contained within the dot.

Alchemy:

The word 'alchemist' comes from 'alchemy', originating in Khem, Egypt. It is the chemistry of God, AL-CHEMY. Alchemy is the perfection of body and soul, the elixir of life and eternal youth. Active since ancient times, alchemists could be considered very early chemists because of their work trying to transform base metals into gold. Alchemists could also be considered wizards, because they attempted to make special elixirs that would give everlasting life and cure sickness. This is the origin of Merlin of King Arthur legend, which is code for our own inner wizardry and alchemy. In planetary terms, the seven metals of alchemy relate to the seven visible planets, as follows:

Saturn = Lead (Black)

Jupiter = Tin

Moon = Silver (White)

Mercury = Mercury

Mars = Iron (Red)

Venus = Copper

Sun = Gold

Black (Saturn) is the first stage of magnum opus (great work) to the philosopher's stone (Gold/Sun), taking us through the 9 divisions of Alchemy + Azoth, which is the Eternal Fire/Krestos = 10. When blackness disappears (Saturn – also symbolised by black robes worn by the Saturnalian brotherhoods), white appears, which gives us the marriage of Heaven and Earth (Union of Opposites) and the complete removal of separation. This is symbolised on the priest's dog collar and also the white column of smoke when a new Pope is elected at the Vatican. That column is a connection between Earth and Heaven. Alchemy is the transmutation from lead (lower self) to gold (higher self).

The alchemical symbol of Gold is also illustrated by this aerial view of Stonehenge:

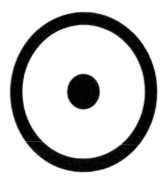

(Alchemical symbol of Gold and Stonehenge)

The higher levels of the Church know the truth of these stories and characters. By the time that history gets to the Christ story, the exact same story has been used many times before. Egypt is one such example, with Isis and Horus being the prerequisite for Mary and Jesus.

The alchemy of the divine androgyny is at the foremost of alchemical ascension, the concept of lead to gold (Unconscious to Conscious), by changing the Atomic number. Everything in creation is a fusion, an intercourse, and this is the Power of Creation which can only be achieved by the masculine and feminine 50/50 balance. *'Aurum Nostrum Non Est Aurum Vulgi'* translated as *'Our Gold Is Not Common Gold'* is an Alchemist saying. It is the Krestos (Fire) that can incarnate within the human being, and those who earn this sacred gift can then be called Christ. This is achieved by worship, which really means workship, in other words, working on our own vessels.

Through the three essences - Mercury, Sulphur, and Salt - we get salvation. Salt gives us the word 'salvation' and resides within our saline environment, the body. Our sexual fire (Krestos/Christ) is clothed within Salt, and it needs to be extracted by transmutation within ourselves to become pure.

Therefore, we are our own salvation!

This is the magnum opus of alchemy, the philosopher's stone.

The philosopher's stone, more properly philosophers' stone or stone of the philosophers (Latin: lapis philosophorum), is a legendary alchemical substance capable of turning base metals, such as mercury, into gold (chrysopoeia, from the Greek χρυσός khrusos, (gold), and ποιεῖν poiēin, (to make)) or silver. It is also called the elixir of life, useful for rejuvenation and for achieving immortality. For many centuries, it was the most sought goal in alchemy. The philosophers' stone was the central symbol of the mystical terminology of alchemy, symbolising perfection at its finest, enlightenment, and heavenly bliss. Efforts to discover the philosophers' stone were known as the 'Magnum Opus' (Great Work).

We can see that something is being hidden from us with documented historical statements such as these:

"It has served us well, this myth of Christ" – Pope Leo X

"Jesus is metaphorical, not literal" – Pope Francis (current Pope at the time of writing)

"We just feel that Jesus is not coming back by the looks of it" – Cardinal Giorgio Salvadore

I will detail many things throughout this book that show just who these characters really are.

I also make many references to chakras and Kundalini throughout the chapters, so I will now define what these are.

Chakras:

The seven main chakras are the energy centres in our bodies in which energy flows through up the spinal column (Jacob's Ladder).

(Human Chakra system)

They are:

The root chakra

The sacral chakra

The solar plexus chakra

The heart chakra

The throat chakra

The third-eye chakra

The crown chakra

But spiritually, this is much wider. There are also musical chakras and they refer to two systems: one with eight chakras, and one with twelve. The first corresponds to the notes of a western scale, the other to including all the half tones. The eight chakra system is similar to the yogic and is said to follow from the 3D egg of life. They are related to survival, physical, or sexual contact, control, the heart, sound, geometry, spirit, and the octave above the head. Between the 3rd and 4th and the 7th and 8th, there are 'walls', or half steps.

The void comes between the 4th and 5th, separating the lower female from the upper male chakras. The locations are only roughly the same as the yogic ones; in particular, the 6th is at the forehead, while the 7th is in the centre of the head. The 8th, over the head, is the base of the next 'dimensional level'.

The twelve chakra system posits equally spaced centres, averaging 7.23 cm apart, 7.23cm is also the wavelength of the chant OM in Hinduism. These correspond respectively to the perineum, the ovaries, the navel, the solar plexus, the sternum, the second heart, Adam's apple, chin, tip of nose, eyes, third eye, crown, and over the head. Each chakra has five sub-chakras (e.g. the clitoris or penis, the vagina or scrotum, the perineum, the anus, the sacrum). The channels are said to rotate by 90 degrees between each chakra, thus spiralling up the spine. The 5th chakra is where the second revolution starts and is special because it is the seat of the Christ consciousness.

Kundalini:

Kundalini is a Sanskrit term that literally means 'coiled one'. In spiritual circles, this term represents the primal force that lies *coiled* at the base of one's spine. Yoga poses, controlled breathing, and meditation provide a means to awaken the Kundalini and channel its enlightening force upward. As Kundalini force rises, it destroys the lower chakras, known as Sodom and Gomorrah, during its sometimes rapid transit from the base of the spine. This is the destruction, by fire, of the two biblical cities, two cities near to and covered by the Dead Sea (also known as the Salt Sea) situated at the base of the spine, which is fed by the river Jordan (the spinal fluid); 'Jordan' meaning 'to descend'. 'Gomorrah' means 'submersion'. The term 'sodomy' is relevant to this.

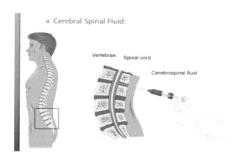

(Region of the river Jordan/Dead Sea)

Incidentally, I have personally seen Kundalini energy, and it is what I would describe as a white chemical faceless serpent fire. It is also known as the serpent/dragon, which is also mentioned frequently throughout the chapters. This is also relevant in the Quetzlecoatl worship in South America. 'Quetzlecoatl' means 'precious serpent', also known as 'Kukulcan', which derives from KU (sacred), KUL = coccyx, and CAN which means 'serpent'. In other words, it is the serpent at the base of the spine, which is code for Kundalini. In Hinduism, we have the Kumara, and 'Kumara' means 'androgynous serpent'!

The serpent is pinnacle in ancient wisdoms and is the symbol of such.

INTRODUCTION:
A WORLD OF MYSTERY

In any of the world's religions or ancient mysteries, there are the public levels of understanding and there are the mystical levels of understanding, whether that is Islam and Sufism, Christianity and Mithraism, or Judaism and the Kabballah, and so on. The Bible can enslave you or enlighten you, but that depends purely upon you and at which level you wish to interpret it. I will be reciting much of the Bible throughout this book, as it is the most read and most influential book in the history of man, a book that hides the information in cryptogram form that I am discussing in this book.

The student of esotericism discovers early on that the ancients often resorted to various blinds to conceal the true interpretations of their mysteries. The English word 'faith' is thought to date from 1200–1250, from the middle English 'feith', via Anglo-French 'fed', Old French 'feid', 'feit' from Latin 'fidem', accusative of 'fidēs' (trust), akin to 'fidere' (to trust), and can you trust at face value those who wrote the Bible? No!

The Bible is written in what is called allegory, meaning that the words that are written and what they mean are two different facts. One is done to conceal esoteric (hidden inner) meanings from the profane (people who do not research/uninitiated) so they are unaware of its true meaning. The other is done to honour truth that these allegorical words cleverly contain.

If you consider such statements as *"Thou shalt have no other gods before me",* then you can see that the worship of Jesus is a clear breach of this first commandment. Worship actually derives from

'Work-Ship' which indicates working on your own vessel.

I have never stated that Christ does not exist. I state that Christ exists in a way not known and certainly not the way in which we have been taught. I have never stated that God does not exist. There is clearly a mathematical and geometric consciousness, an invisible force that can create a numerically-programmed universe. Pythagoras himself once proclaimed that *"All Is Number".*

But, as a trained investigator, when you see parts of a story that have flaws and don't add up, then you bring into question the whole version of events. Many aspects of what we are told is biblical truth, and even ancient cultural historical repetition have these flaws, therefore all must be subsequently questioned. The truth does not have such flaws. Truth has a firm and solid base that does not sway.

When you take the time to look and make an effort to see, you begin to see that there is a much deeper meaning to what is being said at superficial levels, and therefore the real truth is being concealed from all but a select few who understand the true mysteries. The Church is misinterpreting and misunderstanding the true meanings of the scriptures, and scholars are misrepresenting the truth of our famous monuments and monoliths.

The Bible is full of parables, and a parable is a story that contains a spiritual lesson, however, the story has been taught and believed as truth and the spiritual lesson has been completely missed! This makes a huge difference to the real translation and meaning of the content.

When you research deeply enough, you begin to realise that the Bible is a cryptogram, a book of codes and metaphors that hide a secret truth, visible to only those with the eyes that can see and the ears that can hear. It is about interpretation, and only the select few initiates can interpret the symbols and codes correctly, therefore seeing the true mystical teachings. Initiates are people who have been introduced to the mysteries of some field or activity. They are enlightened people, chosen to be so. At birth, the divine mind goes to sleep identifying with the 5 senses. The path of awakening is giving birth to the concept of the self being God. This is the virgin birth of divine consciousness. Our light wanted to be known, therefore it polarised itself in order to see and know itself, which is duality.

The secret teachings are about the 'self' and once you learn about self, you learn about God and Christ and all other biblical characters and stories because, as you will see throughout this book, they are all are a metaphor for self and were never real people. This is a bitter pill to swallow for many but, being realistic, humanity needs to take another look at belief systems and history whose explanation has not changed much in thousands of years if it wishes to advance itself as a race of beings.

No outside saviour is coming from the clouds on a white horse. We are our own saviours and only we can save ourselves, to look without instead of within is a ply to prevent you from learning about self, the place where all should be focused. Incidentally, a white horse is symbolic of a connection to a higher place, hence why there are so many white chalk horses upon hills around the world, especially in the UK. This also includes the unicorn with its horn, which is the energy spiral of the third eye.

There is no such thing as Sin or Hell, they are the technique of reward or punishment to ensure compliance with a certain dogmatic teaching and they have worked – perfectly!

In the religious sense, a sin is described as an immoral act considered to be a transgression against the divine laws which are contained in sacred religious texts. The English word 'sin' means to "*miss the mark*".

It is derived from the biblical Greek New Testament ἀμαρτία hamartia "*sin*"; missing the mark (failure or error) which is derived from the Hebrew Hata – "*sin*". It is a word that originates in archery and literally refers to missing the "gold" at the "*centre of a target,*" not hitting the target – i.e. to "m*iss the mark*". This is what is really meant by the biblical passage in John 8:7, "*let he who is without sin cast the first stone*".

So what does that really mean? Well, let's break it down into bite sizes. 'He without sin', the Gnostic with knowledge, who has hit the mark of enlightenment, 'cast' which comes from the Hebrew word 'yadah/yada' which means know or knowing (knowledge), 'the first' is the most important, 'stone' which is the foundation stone and the stone of wisdom the pineal gland. In other words, the Gnostic (Wiseman of knowledge) knows the knowledge of the stone.

In this story, it talks about a prostitute being the subject and this, of course, takes us into lower sexual desire which is satanic consciousness, but more on this in a later chapter. This Gold, the alchemists' philosopher's stone, will be expanded upon throughout the book. 'Philosopher' comes from 'philosophy', which means 'wisdom' or the study of knowledge and wisdom, therefore the philosopher's stone is the stone of wisdom, or the wisdom stone. The foundation stone is also a reference to the pineal gland, which is also mentioned periodically throughout the book.

So, when we sin, we often and still do miss the "*gold mark*" at the centre of a target of Golgotha ('*place of the skull' where Jesus was 'crucified'*) because we are not complete in Christ, who is in the head, the temple.

It is said in 1 Corinthians 11:3; *"But I want you to understand that Christ is the head of every man, and the man is the head of a woman, and God is the head of Christ."* This will become more apparent to you as we move through the book.

This error in not knowing what Christ really is and not truly using reason and our heads leads us to "miss the mark or sin" when we think and act.

Therefore, many of us kill our brother *"Able or Ability"* and miss the mark and, as such, we carry the *"Mark of Cain"* (Cainites), the life of immorality and Sin, not thinking before we act. The name Cain means *'possessed'*. Those who possess the gnosis (Knowledge) can never Sin, because they have hit the mark, the knowledge.

You are about to be taken on a journey of Gnostic revelation, a journey that is presented to you by a former police investigator who has deciphered an esoteric code that changes the teachings of all religions.

In truth, all religions have the same origin at their mystical levels, hidden by different names and places, but nevertheless they all refer to the same esoteric subject matter, the SELF!

"Signs and symbols rule the world, not words, nor laws" – Confucius

What you are about to be told was only ever meant for the initiates of the Mystery Schools, the chosen students of Gnostic and Kabbalistic knowledge. Knowledge is hidden by symbols, metaphors, and parables in order to keep it concealed to everyone other than those with the knowledge of correct interpretation of the mystical and sacred wisdom.

This book is your own *'Star of Bethlehem'* that *'Wise-Men'* follow in order to find their own Christ within, their own divine realisation.

The Star of Bethlehem, as you will see later, is the Pentagram, the symbol of many Mystery Schools that King Herod could not see or find as he, a symbolic representation of the general population, lacked the wisdom to see the sacred knowledge. Esoterically it symbolizes the "Law of Fives", Penta-gram (Penta = five!). In Hebrew it is Van = Nail = the Nails that fixed Christ to the cross (3 nails) = the three purification's of iron and fire, which is the separation of the impure from the pure in Alchemy. It is code for consciousness.

The Kabbalists state that the Bible is a cryptogram, a book of codes, and that those who decipher the codes will be met by spiritual forces of transmutation. This is correct, and I speak from personal experience of those forces.

Everything is a frequency, and you can only see what you are tuned into. It is now time to raise our frequency and expand our visible spectrum or, in computer jargon, expand our bandwidth which is ready and waiting for us all to do within our dormant protein-based DNA that science wrongly and mistakenly calls 'junk DNA'.

"Father forgive them for they know not what they do" (Luke 23:34) is code for 'they do not know the meanings of the hidden teachings'. This leads to confusion, the tower of Babel, 'babel' meaning 'confused', and the lack of understanding of what Christ really is leads to such confusion. But those who understand the mysteries and their true teachings tower over the unknowing members of society, the masses. 'Babel' derives from *"Ba"* the gate, of *"Bel"* the Sun-Christ ('Bel' also gives us 'Bell' as in Church bell). Babel is the gate of the Sun-Christ, which is the pineal gland, and to miss this bullseye is to miss the mark which is sin (I will go into this later). The Watchtower is, of course, also the magazine of the same name of the Jehovah's witnesses for this reason, unbeknownst to them.

There are four levels of humans who are considered inferior;

Instinctual human being (Those who inherited their religion – from parents etc.)

Emotional human being (People that are emotionally centred, they are emotional Christians)

Intellectual human being (They are very intellectual, they explain the Bible, even memorise it)

Equilibrated human being (The equilibrated man follows the right path - you are not identified, you enter into any religion, because you understand that all religions are to do with creation). The Kingdom of Heaven has nothing to do with beliefs; it is to do with creation.

The first thing that we have to create is within us, and is called the Inner Jesus Christ.

"These three levels of humans do not understand each other. The instinctual level does not understand the intellectual. The emotional level does not understand the intellectual. The intellectual level does not understand the emotional." - Samael Aun Weor

The human beings of the first, second, and third level constitute the circle of the confusion of tongues, the Tower of Babel. The Tower of Babel is symbolic of humanity and not a real place. If you identify with any of those levels - intellectual, emotional, instinctual - you enter into the confusion of tongues, because they are contradictory. They have many wrong interpretations of what is written in their religious scriptures.

Many ancient symbols are telling us this in an esoteric way. The crown below (serpent) is the symbol of mastery and the union that takes place within the student when the life forces are lifted to the brain - The Masters of Wisdom, all Initiates into the Sacred Mysteries, are called Nagas, or Serpents of Wisdom. The serpent is the vehicle to messianic consciousness.

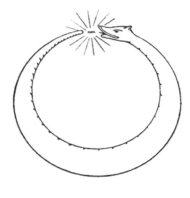

(The Serpent)

The fire of the gods was given to them, in their belief systems, by Prometheus, and that fire is knowledge and wisdom, therefore the wisdom of the gods.

The writers of these religious scriptures (scripts) knew full well that they were creating a multi-tiered belief system to keep sacred knowledge away from the general population, who they deemed unworthy of such wisdom. They continue to teach the same way week after week, year after year, and generation after generation. When I was a police officer and stood before the judge in court, which was a frequent event, I was always asked this question, *"When did you make your evidential notes, Officer?"* In order for my evidence to be used in court, the evidence needed to be written straight after the event or as soon after as practicable, as this way it was a fresh and accurate account of what had occurred.

If I had not documented the evidence until even just a few hours after the event, it may have resulted in that evidence not being accepted as truth. If, in the case of evidence allegedly written in the Bible whereby the account was written 400 years after the event, such as the Jesus story, then you can imagine what would have been said by the court. Yet we accept this as evidence at face value without question, because we are programmed to conform and believe what we are told to believe and without challenge of question.

The Bible is a division of the Hebrew Scriptures, and therefore the Kabbalah is a foundation stone to understanding its mystical teachings. I will introduce you to the Kabbalah shortly. It is also important to understand alchemy, Gods chemistry, the fusion between man and God, which will also feature frequently throughout the book. The subjects covered in this book, taught at their intended level of understanding, will give you a higher consciousness and, by that, I mean a mystical awareness of the mysteries. It is turning lead to gold, unconscious to conscious, by changing the atomic number. Everything in creation is a fusion, an intercourse of opposites. This is also our power of creation. And by balance of opposites, it means the complete removal of separation and transmutation into non-duality. This gives us tantric knowledge of sexuality, which features heavily in alchemy and religion.

The human mind, according to George Friedrich Hegel, a 19th century German philosopher, cannot understand unless things are split into polar opposites such as black and white, left and right, and so on. This is known as the 'Hegelian Dialect'. We must rise above duality.

If you want to understand the mystical codes of the Bible and alike, you need to understand the minds of those responsible for the encryption and their belief systems, and this is something that I have done. I have gone to the depth of the mystical source and I have learned to speak their language. This book goes to the very heart of those coded systems of hidden knowledge. If biblical characters didn't exist, and I provide evidence in this book to suggest that they didn't, then biblical events didn't happen either. But the stories must be referring to something, and that something is a metaphorical truth hidden behind those stories. And this is where we should be looking.

The codes and hidden messages give you a completely different interpretation of the scriptures, namely the truth of their meanings!

For example, the word 'Priest' derives from the Hebrew word 'Magush', which is also where we get the word 'Magi' or 'magician'. Therefore, the early Priests were alchemists and magicians. Someone recently said to me that they were confused, as they had seen things on a church, such as a griffin, that didn't belong there. I replied that it does belong there if you understand what it means. The griffin, which is a creature that is half lion and half eagle, is alchemical code for the rose coloured blood of the lion mixed with the gluten of the eagle, in other words, sulphur and mercury. The Gargoyle on the Church is a vivid reminder that the state in which man lives does not dictate his divinity. In alchemy the lion is gold and the winged serpent is duality. The winged serpent became the dragon which has the same symbology.

Wings are symbolic of the hidden potential to vanquish base characteristics (depravity) and show man's capacity to rise above and master his potential.

What we are is not what we have to be!

Alchemy deals with the transmutation of self, and it stems from Ancient Egypt which was originally called 'Khem', from where the word 'alchemy' derives. 'Al' was later added to indicate god, so therefore alchemy is god's chemistry. In the pyramid of Teotihuacán in 2015, Mercury was found beneath it and scholars are still pondering over its meaning. It is alchemy. Teotihuacán means 'City of the Gods' but really, this means the city where men become Gods. Become Gods through alchemy.

It is a book that will challenge your deepest held belief or knowledge of something that many have held onto for so long that it might release you from the slavery of cognitive dissonance, or even the unseen prison of misunderstanding.

Truth is truth in whatever language we use, and can be clearly recognised as such if we have an open mind. The mind is pinnacle, as it is the seat of our consciousness and where we have the third eye, which is the Vatika, from where we get the word 'Vatican'. 'Tika' means third eye, and also gives us the Mayan pyramids in Tikal (Tika). This is why there are so many pinecone statues within the Vatican City, as pinecone gives us the word 'pineal'. "*If thine eye be single, thy body will be full of light*" which is reference to the pineal gland, the single cyclopean eye, the third eye of spiritual sight. It is how Jesus can cure the blind, because the blindness referred to here is ignorance and the knowledge of the pineal gland can remove ignorance, thus curing blindness. The pineal gland is also the mountain of Peniel, where Jacob fought the angel and saw the face of God. The pineal gland is known as the eye and the face of God. This particular biblical story was one of consciousness, as are the majority.

This book is intended to give you an insight into the things that are taught to the elect secretly by religions and ancient mystery school cultures.

The Bible is a cryptogram, a book of codes that conceal a message! Even when we add the books of both the Old Testament (39) and the New Testament (27), it equals 66. In the Kaballah, the number 66 is the numerical value of the wheel (Gilgal), which has relevance to Ezekiel's vision of the chariot.

(Ezekiel's Vision of the Chariot)

The chariot, or wheel, as you will see later, is a reference to higher consciousness. 'Gilgal' also gives us Google, the modern day computer search engine, whereby we can obtain knowledge.

It is said within the Kaballah that *'one should not teach the Act of the Chariot to an individual, unless he is wise and can understand the implications himself'.*

It is mysticism, allegorical, and symbolic significance that transcends human understanding. It is important to realise that the Kabbalah is more about losing ourselves than about finding, becoming more other-centred and less ego-centred. The literal translation of the word 'Kabbalah' is 'that which is received'. To receive, we must be receptive. We must open ourselves, creating a vessel in which to absorb that which we wish to understand or grasp and, in turn, we can then understand the Kabbalah. To open the self to a higher reality, to view the spirit within the matter, to raise our consciousness to the point where our perception of reality is completely changed and the divine within all creation is revealed. And, of course, Moses received the law of God on the mountain and 'receive' in Hebrew is 'Kibel', which is where we get the word 'Kabballah'.

This book will enlighten you with the secrets of the Church, the Kabballah, the Gnostics, and the Alchemists, showing you that the true essence of all is YOU!

This is a secret that is widely known and understood within the Mystery Schools, with their epicentre emanating from Ancient Egypt and spreading throughout the world into the Kabbalah and even Ancient Greece, whose philosophers were Egyptian Mystery School initiates, spending many years there. Pythagoras, for example, spent 22 years as an initiate in Egypt.

By reading this book, you will become one of the biblical 144:000, which never meant the amount of people that would be with Christ in Heaven as Jehovah's witnesses proclaim, as they have also misunderstood the knowledge. 144:000 gives us a coded message, which is 1+4+4+0+0+0=9. 9 is the number of completion and esoteric man and the number of consciousness in mysticism.

This is how we can be with Christ in Heaven as it means consciousness within the mind, which is Heaven. This formula is used numerous times with the same meaning, such as the 12 tribes of Israel that originate from the 12 sons of Jacob, which gives us 12x12=144.

The 6 days of creation equate to 144 hours and there are 1440 minutes to every day. Israel was in bondage in Egypt for 400 years. 1 biblical year = 360 days, 400 years * 360 days/year = 144,000 days, 360 or 3+6+0 = 9 and 144 or 1+4+4 = 9 and so on. Even the pyramids of Egypt have relevance to this number. It is also no coincidence that the Great Pyramid had 144,000 outer casing stones and in Gemetria, the numerical value of letters and words, 144 is light. 144 is the secret key and concept of light itself. The human third eye has a hertz frequency of, you guessed it, 144 hertz. The 144,000 outer cased limestones caused the pyramid to gleam like a "light" in the bright Sun and could be seen for many miles. Limestone (and its quartz frequencies) also line up with Christ Consciousness! Limestone also has the same approximate wavelength as Gold, which is the colour of enlightenment. Limestone and Gold are both around 590 NM (Nanometres).

Quartz is a mineral composed of silicon and oxygen atoms in a continuous framework of SiO_4 silicon–oxygen tetrahedral (pyramid shape), with each oxygen being shared between two tetrahedrons, giving an overall chemical formula of SiO_2. Quartz is the second most abundant mineral in Earth's continental crust, behind feldspar.

In the first 3 gospels, the term 'King of the Jews' is used 12 times, which gives us 3x12 = 36. 36 is the number of the initiation, the number of knocks of the hammer that nailed Christ to the cross and, according to Edgar Cayce, it is the age that Joseph took Mary as his wife. In Chinese astrology, there are 36 beneficial stars and 72 malefic stars, with their sum giving us 108. This is the number of the inner dimensions of the pentagram, and 108 is within the center of a 5-sided regular polygon (a regular pentagon). The sum of the interior angles of a polygon is gotten by the formula - sum of interior angels (= numbers of sides) * 180. For a 5-sided polygon (pentagon), this is (5-2)*180 = 3*180=540. Since all 5 angles of a regular pentagon are equal, each interior angle of the regular pentagon is 108. 36 degrees is also the interior angle of each of the tips of the pentagram and I mention the pentagram a number of times during this book for good esoteric reason.

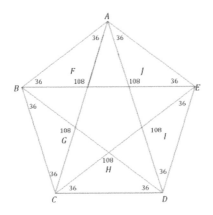

(Pentagram Angles)

The distance between the Earth and the Sun is approximately 108 times the Sun's diameter. The diameter of the Sun is about 108 times the Earth's diameter. And the distance between the Earth and the Moon is 108 times the Moon's diameter. Every 8 years, Venus orbits the Sun in the shape of a pentagram.

The Kabballah is rife with numerology.

You are about to enter the true Kingdom of God, and you are about to tune into a new and higher frequency of truth. You are about to be saved which, in Gnosis, is those who have learned to rise above their lower mind and lower emotions.

Here is your key to the truth... That truth is YOU.

These ancient and mystical secrets will soon be known by you.

What is alchemy?

The word 'alchemist' comes from 'alchemy', originating in Khem, Egypt. It is the chemistry of God, AL-CHEMY. Alchemy is the perfection of body and soul, the elixir of life and eternal youth. Active since ancient times, alchemists could be considered very early chemists because of their work trying to transform base metals into gold. Alchemists could also be considered wizards, because they attempted to make special elixirs that would give everlasting life and cure sickness. This is the origin of Merlin of King Arthur legend, which is code for our own inner wizardry and alchemy. In planetary terms, the seven metals of alchemy relate to the seven visible planets, as follows:

Saturn = Lead (Black)

Jupiter = Tin

Moon = Silver (White)

Mercury = Mercury

Mars = Iron (Red)

Venus = Copper

Sun = Gold

Black (Saturn) is the first stage of magnum opus (great work) to the philosopher's stone (Gold/Sun), taking us through the 9 divisions of Alchemy + Azoth which is the Eternal Fire/Krestos = 10. When blackness disappears (Saturn – also symbolised by black robes worn by the Saturnalian brotherhoods), white appears, which gives us the marriage of Heaven and Earth (Union of Opposites) and the complete removal of separation. This is symbolised on the priest's dog collar and also the white column of smoke when a new Pope is elected at the Vatican. That column is a connection between Earth and Heaven. Alchemy is the transmutation from lead (lower self) to gold (higher self).

The higher levels of the Church know the truth of these stories and characters. By the time that history gets to the Christ story, the exact same story has been used many times before. Egypt is one such example, with Isis and Horus being the prerequisite for Mary and Jesus.

The alchemy of the divine androgyny is at the foremost of alchemical ascension, the concept of lead to gold (Unconscious to Conscious), by changing the Atomic number. Everything in creation is a fusion, an intercourse, and this is the Power of Creation which can only be achieved by the masculine and feminine 50/50 balance. 'Aurum Nostrum Non Est Aurum Vulgi' translated as 'Our Gold Is Not Common Gold' is an Alchemist saying. It is the Krestos (Fire) that can incarnate within the human being, and those who earn this sacred gift can then be called Christ. This is achieved by worship, which really means 'workship', in other words, working on our own vessels.

Through the three essences - Mercury, Sulphur, and Salt - we get salvation. Salt gives us the word 'salvation' and resides within our saline environment, the body. Our sexual fire (Krestos/Christ) is clothed within Salt, and it needs to be extracted by transmutation within ourselves to become pure.

Therefore, we are our own salvation!

This is the magnum opus of alchemy; the philosopher's stone.

The philosopher's stone, more properly philosophers' stone or stone of the philosophers (Latin: lapis philosophorum), is a legendary alchemical substance capable of turning base metals, such as mercury, into gold (chrysopoeia, from the Greek χρυσός khrusos, (gold), and ποιεῖν poiēin, (to make)) or silver. It is also called the elixir of life, useful for rejuvenation and for achieving immortality. For many centuries, it was the most sought goal in alchemy. The philosopher's stone was the central symbol of the mystical terminology of alchemy, symbolising perfection at its finest, enlightenment, and heavenly bliss. Efforts to discover the philosopher's stone were known as the 'Magnum Opus' (Great Work).

Why Lot's Wife Turned Into Salt...

Alchemy is an important process for the initiates, the inner chemical process from first spirit to the Philosopher's Stone, the Gold of Alchemical Ascension. It is inner illumination and wisdom.

The word 'alchemy', as with 'chemistry', derives from Khem, which is the name for Egypt. It was a form of inner magic used in Ancient Egypt and forms the basis of the pyramid shape.

The pyramid shape is the three essences of alchemy, the three headed dragon, which are salt, sulphur, and mercury that form a trinity, the law of the triangle. The gold pyramid capstone at the top of the great pyramid indicates the completion of magnum opus, the great work... It is an alchemy term and a term also used by the Kabbalah, which is a corrupted version of Egyptian knowledge of self.

Merlin of King Arthur fame is also a metaphor for our inner

wizardry and alchemy, the magical process of turning base metals into gold. It is Azoth or, biblically, the 'Alpha and Omega'.

The base of the pyramid faces in the direction of the 4 cardinal points which are also the 4 corners and the 4 elements or, if you are a Jehovah's witness, the watchtower, your magazine name! The Cardinal's of the church represent the four, which is the material, which we have to surpass to reach the five, the ether.

That then leads us onto universal energy that is divided into 4 frequencies, and gives us the 4 elements of the body and the cosmos.

This inner process is also spoken about in the likes of the Bible with the story of Lot's wife turning into salt as she looked back at Sodom.

The destruction of the biblical Sodom and Gomorrah is really a metaphor for the lower chakras engulfed in the fire of Kundalini energy as it rises up the spine (Jacob's ladder). The lower chakras are the place of lower desires and this is why the Bible tells us these lands were destroyed by fire - it is purely allegorical.

It is the divine spark within, the alchemical combustion.

But what about Lot's wife turning into salt?

It is a metaphor for alchemy and its inner processes.

Salt in alchemy is the physical body, and it is also where we get the true meaning of biblical 'salvation' which derives from 'Sal' meaning 'salt'! 'Yeshua' means 'salvation', and therefore we are our own salvation.

The salt is what remains of the body after alchemical combustion, it is the corporeal (body) substance that survived the death in order to re-inaugurate into a new life, an internal resurrection.

It is part of the Tria Prima process of alchemy. This divine spark is lord of the body.

What is a God? In monotheistic thought, God is conceived of as the Supreme Being, creator deity, and principal object of faith. God is usually conceived as being omniscient, omnipotent, and omnipresent, and as having an eternal and necessary existence. These attributes are used either in way of analogy or are taken literally. God is most often held to be incorporeal. Incorporeality and corporeality of God are related to conceptions of transcendence and immanence of God, with positions of synthesis such as the "immanent transcendence".

In certain other religions, God is a superhuman being or spirit worshipped as having power over nature or human fortunes, a deity. It can be as simple as a greatly admired or influential person or a thing of worship. The word 'God' originated from the English word 'good'. It points to the divine goodness of the Supreme Being who created the universe. For centuries, English speakers believed that God is called this because he is good. Some people believe that extra-terrestrials are Gods and that they even created the modern day human, the homosapien. A God can be something as simple as the worship of a pop-idol admiring their pop poster on your wall.

But what this book will show you is that you are in fact God. You are an aspect of what is God because you are a miniature universe, and therefore an image of creation itself, albeit a smaller version of that creation as a whole.

Our ancient ancestors left clues within the most famous landmarks of Earth, in their monoliths and great enduring monuments, and even religious scriptures and mythical locations, such as Atlantis and Lemuria. They were transmuting themselves into a higher type of human by certain rituals and practises such as alchemy, and they had a direct connection to the stars and other planets that created a network and knowledge base that they all shared. Therefore, contrary to mainstream history that tells you that ancient cultures were uncivilised and separate from other civilisations, they were closely connected to each other by knowledge and advanced know-how of the greater beyond.

If you and I were describing the same event, we would most likely use different terminology to describe it; you may say red and I may say crimson, but we are talking about the same thing. The ancient code that I have found is the same scenario, many ways of describing the same things. You may say Jehovah or Allah or Yahweh but the base and the origins are the same, they are the same thing.

Modern science, or what we deem to be modern science, is an ancient knowledge and an ancient know-how. It isn't new at all. But it is important to know that these secrets were hidden behind allegories, and an allegory is a story that, when interpreted correctly, reveals a hidden meaning.

Humans are not from Earth, as I will show you later, and our DNA is yet to be fully activated. Human DNA is a 3 billion letter code, a message within the smaller universe inside of us. What happens when the key that unlocks us is turned and by whom will it be turned? And that 3 billion letter code does not include our protein-based DNA which science calls junk DNA but, in reality, it is a dormant code and not junk. In our nucleotides, A-T and G-C always attached and align.

We are greatness unrealised and we are the fabric of space and the universe. We live on in organic form from stars that lived as glowing gas and heat. They died and we were born from them. We became youngsters or young-stars. When we die physically, our essence will also live on in another guise, somewhere as something (some-thing).

What if the stars that we see each and every night are really Suns for orbiting planets that we cannot see? What if those planets contain life right on our doorstep? What if ancient monoliths and monuments were used to communicate with our galactic neighbours and are even hiding messages from other races themselves? Earth humans are really from the Orion Nebula and are therefore actually the visitors here on Earth. In which case, are humans not the real aliens?

I am about to unlock the mysteries of the advanced ancient sages (Sagittarius), hermetics, and hierophants, and from all around the world I will connect these ancient wise-ones who came from the stars and returned to the stars.

Through such practices as alchemy, they were able to transform and transmute. Through enlightened consciousness they were shown the way. The elder race of man has left the tools for us to follow in their path.

Will we set our course back to Orion, the gateway of man?

ONE

THE ELDER RACE OF MAN: HUMANS ARE NOT FROM EARTH

Universe means one verse, and a verse is a metrical rhythm. Metrical relates to the metre, which relates to mathematics. That universe is made up of three components, proton (positive), electron (negative), and the neutron (neutral). Rhythm relates to sound and, within the universe, the nodes of standing waves dictate the location of stars and planets, making them the exact distance that they need to be away from each other. This falls within Einstein's Theory of Relativity, where all is reliant upon each other, all locked into each other's orbit at the exact correct distance. His famous $E=MC^2$ is telling us of the universal powerhouse which is energy in which E represents units of energy, M represents units of mass, and C^2 is the speed of light squared. Because the speed of light is a very large number, it is multiplied by itself. The equation points out how a small amount of matter can release a huge amount of energy, as in a nuclear reaction.

The physical finite world is governed by finite fractals (duplication) and one of the most remarkable mathematical codes is the Mandelbrot set, a complex series of numbers that will not deviate and can only be replicated by computer. It is a complex series that is self-replicating according to some predetermined rule. It creates a finite mathematical equation of ZN, the set of complex numbers C for which the iteration $ZN+1 = ZN2 + C$ producing finite ZN for all N when started at $Z0 = 0$ duplicating forever in the nonphysical world. The Mandelbrot set has also appeared as a crop circle.

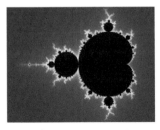

(Mandelbrot Set)

Within the mass of the universe, we have galaxies and, within galaxies, there are billions of stars. One of those stars is that bright, burning ball of gas we see each day called the solar Sun. The word 'Sun' derives from 'sonic' or 'sound', and the Hindu word for 'Sun' is 'Om', which they believed to be the primordial sound that created the universe. Around our Sun, there are planets that orbit making up the solar system, a system meaning to work together. One of those planets is highly significant to us and that planet is Earth, our current home planet. On Earth, there are countries and, within those countries, there are regions. Within those regions, there is a building and, within that building, there is a room that contains someone reading this book. That person is you!

You are the universal geometry, the golden ratio, and you are a miniature universe. Within your body, there is an even smaller universe called cells and atoms that mimic the grand celestial machine above you. Your electrons orbit the nucleus of your atoms, as do the planets of the solar system orbit the Sun.

Our atoms are 99.999999999999 per cent empty space, which results in a time-space continuum within our genes. Our genetic code is a set of rules used by cells to translate information encoded within our genes, and our genetic make-up has four nucleotides that have 64 combinations (64 keys of Enoch). Ribosomes are our genetic translators. We all draw from our own gene pool, and dependent upon how those genes cross one another determines our human appearance, and this is why there are so many different looking races on Earth and this is of course also applicable to races outside of Earth. Human languages did not appear coincidentally, but are a reflection of our inherent DNA, and some scientists believe that the human DNA is arranged in such a precise way that it reveals a set of arithmetic patterns. Some Russian scientists say that DNA follows the same rules as all our human languages. Therefore, words are genetics turned into an audible sound.

They found that the alkaline of our DNA follows a regular grammar and do have set rules just like our languages. They also say that DNA was created outside of Earth. Scientists in Kazakhstan believe that human DNA is encoded with an alien signal for an ancient extra-terrestrial civilisation, and they refer to this as 'Biological-SETI'. SETI stands for the 'Search for Extra-Terrestrial Intelligence'.

It has been discovered written in the *Sēpher Yaṣîrâh* (which means *'Book of Formation'* or *'Book of Creation'* in Hebrew) text that DNA is encoded in layers like a book, and that the first layer says God/eternal within the body. This is the same in the three root languages of Earth, Hebrew, Sanskrit, and Aramaic. It is a signature of the creator. In 2007, Japanese scientists placed a message within the bacteria of human DNA, and that message was *"E=MC2 in the year 1905"* and that message lasted several generations. They proved that you can store information within genetics for as long as that genome remains intact. With this discovery, it means that you can reverse that message and have direct communication with its code writer.

At this stage, anything beyond the first layer is not known. Life is the elements which are described through words and numbers, also called the periodic table that make up the DNA of our body. There is an ancient understanding of the power of letters which are associated with numbers called Gemetria, and Gemetria has 32 laws that are not deviated from. Gemetria is the numerical value of letters and words. By the arrangements of these component parts, we get this genetic code, which is an internal message. It is also the 32 paths of wisdom of the Hebrew Sephiroth contained within 33 degrees, 33 being the number of divine realisation and 33 features frequently throughout this book.

With that said, the Orion Nebula is the nursery for Earth. You are a dead star from Orion that lives on in you! After, at some point, when you physically part from this world, you will return to the great silence, from where creation began.

Orion gives us 'Or-ion', and an ion is an atom or molecule with a net electric charge due to the gain or loss of an electron. 'Or' is gold, and therefore Orion (Or-ion), or Gold-ion, are electrons that determine the physical properties of matter. You are made of matter (material) and at physical birth you are a youngster, a young-star, from Orion. Dead stars create life and dead stars from Orion create the carbon and oxygen that allows life on Earth. Humans are the carbon footprint widely spoken about. This is created by what is known as the 'Triple Alpha Process (TAP) which is a set of nucleur fusion reactions by which 3 helium – 4 numclei (alpha particles) are transformed into carbon and this is created in the stars. Therefore we are all starseeds through panspermia. Based on the differences between man and all the other species that inhabit the planet, scientists theorise that mankind is not suited to live on this planet. Such examples would be back issues with Earth's powerful gravitational effects, sunburn, and toddlers taking many years to become independent whereas in the animal kingdom their young are instantly ready for life here. There are, of course, many more. When you look at many famous monuments around the world and many not so famous ones, you can see a fascination with Orion and Orion's belt with their obvious alignment to this constellation. Orion is the gateway of man.

(Orion ET in Egypt – Right is enhanced picture)

There are many monuments all around the world that are aligned to the constellation of Orion and this is for the exact same reason: consciousness and its connection to the pineal gland. This proves that these ancient cultures were tapping into the same knowledge base. Here are just a few examples of note:

Teotihuacán

Located in the highlands of central Mexico, 35 miles northeast of present day Mexico City, lies the ruins of the ancient city of Teotihuacán, another marvel of the ancient world with ties to star constellations. Archaeologists and scholars debate the age of the site, although it is generally agreed upon that the city flourished for at least 500 years before it completely collapsed by the 7th century of the Common Era. The city was one of the largest in the world at its peak, with an approximate population of 150,000-200,000 people. Despite the fact that the city predated the Aztecs by several centuries, they called it Teotihuacán, meaning the "Place of the Gods", as they believed that it was the place where the current world was created. Like many sacred sites from the ancient world, the observatories, pyramids, and structures at Teotihuacán are constructed mirroring celestial alignments. The complex at Teotihuacán contains three pyramids, two larger and one smaller, boasting a similarity to the layout of the pyramids at Giza and forming another correlation to the belt of Orion. The Pyramid of the Sun is said to be aligned with the Pleiades, another constellation of great importance in myth and lore that is often connected to the constellation of Orion.

The Hopi are a Native American tribe whose cosmology, monuments, and landscape have a deep connection with the constellation of Orion. For many generations, they built and abandoned villages before settling on an area comprised of three mesas in the north eastern part of Arizona, where they have been for over a thousand years.

The natural structure of the three mesas mirrors are the three stars in the belt of Orion, and it is said that this is why the Hopi chose to settle in this location. They believe this place to be the centre of their universe, where they can make contact with the gods. Furthermore, when connected to other Hopi monuments and landmarks around the southwest, the collective sites are said to map the entire constellation of Orion. The Hopi Indian red and blue star Kachina prophecy also refers to the stars, namely Sirius, as due to what is known as the Doppler effect, when Sirius goes away from the Sun in its solar binary it is red and when it is returning it is blue. This is when the Earth is flooded by the star energy of Sirius and an awakening takes place.

Around 500 miles south of Cairo, on a desolate plain in the eastern region of the Sahara Desert, we will find the mysterious archaeological site known as Nabta Playa. Discovered by a team of scientists in 1974, researchers believe the stones scattered here were once part of a vast ritual centre for an ancient civilisation that thrived from 6400 to 3400 B.C., just before the rise of the Egyptians. Nabta Playa is different; it wasn't a settlement. One of the centre pieces is a circle that has been called the "mini Stonehenge of the desert". For more than three decades, this circular stone structure and its intricate alignment to the stars of the Orion constellation have baffled archaeologists. The builders of Nabta Playa seem to be aware of a level of physics and understandings of mathematics that allowed them to build these structures in relation to the Orion constellation. There are, of course, many more examples of Orion's correlation with ancient monuments.

Wherever we are from in the universe, we have the same pattern of design, but we have different chemical elements that form our appearances and even a different genetic code. We are just aligned to a different star-system.

I will now ask you to look at the stars differently. A star is a celestial body and hot gas that emits its own light and heat, whereas a planet is reflected light, it doesn't have its own light. What if each star that we can see with the naked eye is in fact a Sun, and around that Sun are planets that we cannot see because the reflected light is too far away for us to detect? What we can see as humans depends upon reflected light within the horizontal ovals we call our eyes. If we were to look at our own Sun from outer space, we wouldn't see the planets of our solar system that are lit-up by our Sun. In the universe, there are two forms of light; visible light and invisible light known as dark matter, which I would suggest is cosmic glue that holds all together. A photon, a particle of light, is a messenger particle, and a photon travels at the speed of light, therefore external to time and outside of our time-space continuum. I will deal with time in just a moment. Photons are conscious, something discovered during the 'double slit' experiment whereby the photon behaved differently when being observed, and therefore it knew that it was, in fact, being observed. The photon is the quantum of the electromagnetic field, and the electromagnetic field is a dual charge of electricity and magnetism.

Oscillation within the electromagnetic field gives us light and colour, and when we see the likes of wonderful finite fractals that are lightning strikes, that is the product of sound and its branch of sono-luminescence. This is the emission of short bursts of light from imploding bubbles in a liquid when excited by sound, and when luminescence is excited in a substance by the passage of sound waves through it.

"Our universe is full of lots of weird solar systems" - Sarah Blunt, California Institute of Technology

With this in mind, we could potentially have many races on our doorstep. One of the things that all ancient sites do is point towards the sky. As you will see in a forthcoming chapter, I do not need SETI to tell me that we are being visited; I would even suggest that humanity is, in fact, the alien race here. You will also see that it is my opinion that our elder race of man, from Orion and other star-systems, built the ancient monuments to be used as a key to our enlightenment and this is why there are no records of them being built by the many civilisations that used them; they were taught how to use them by those who placed them there. Stonehenge and Silbury Hill, for example, as you will see later, are aligned to the planet Mars.

So, what is God? To me, the answer to that is God is a mathematical mind that has created a universe of numbers where everything follows a numerical programme. Many people see number sequences time and time again and never give thought to the fact that a numerical universe is talking to them through one of its languages, mathematics. It is quite evident that everything is a programmed code and if you can decipher that code, you can speak another language, a mathematical and genetic language.

For me, this can often be a night-time communication such as this one. I was simply given this (√937) and nothing more.

It was the symbol of the square root (√), and the square root of 937 = 30.6104557 (30.6). 937 is the 13th 'Star Number'. A star number is a central figurate number representing a centred hexagram (6 pointed star). The 13th Star number is as so - 12x12th triangular number +1.

The hexagram represents the ascent towards Godhead (Egyptian terminology for enlightened consciousness) and also represents insight, wisdom, and the magic power within. It is also unity consciousness (hive consciousness).

In nature, the bee creates a honeycomb which is the shape of the hexagram.

The bee is a symbol of Egyptian Royalty, for this reason. Four hours later, with a head that hurt, I had worked out my dream state communication.

UNIVERSAL TIME:

Many say that time is an illusion and that it doesn't exist. We look at a clock each and every day, many times, and we see a numerical representation of the duration of existence, so this is time.

Many say that beyond Earth, time doesn't exist either, especially within the New Age.

The likes of Einstein stated that time is the fourth dimension, noting that time is inseparable from space.

Well, time does exist, and it also exists beyond Earth! And this is how.

The universe is mathematical code and everything adheres to number sequences from which it will not deviate. Time is also mathematics and therefore exists; that is why Einstein possibly proclaimed that time cannot be separated from space, as they are interlinked. Time is a measure of the interval between two events, measured in seconds. The second is defined by the electronic transition of the Cesium atom. The Cesium atom has the vibration of the second.

When we look at the atomic clock, which is a microwave/electron transition frequency within the electromagnetic spectrum of atoms, we see hyper-fine (small) transitions. The second is 1/60th of a minute, 1/3600th of an hour, or 1/86400 of a day, and so on. We measure time by the oscillations of the Cesium atom at zero magnetic fields which gives us the second, the basis of time. Another one of my thoughts is if time is atomic then before the creation of the atom there was no time in existence only infinity.

Time relates to this Cesium measurement and time is mathematical. The atomic number of the cesuim atom is 55 and an atomic number is simply the amount of protons around the nucleus of every atom of that element. 55 relates to gateways and entrances especially in the Kaballah where we have Hei (gate to Binah) and Hei (second Hei, which is the gate from Malchut) and they have values of 50+5. Therefore the cesium atom has 55 protons around the nucleus of each atom. Two electrons in the same space must have opposite spin (spin up & spin down). Cesium energy is the energy difference of two electron spin states on the magnetic field of the nucleus which means you can maximise the number of oscillations between these two states. This creates a magnetic vortex spin which are the wormholes of space and time. Electron spin is what creates magnetism and magnetic vortex spin is what creates wormholes in space and time. 55, in my theorem, is the hidden instructions to create a gap in time and space to travel through by negative spin.

Earth's two poles have a clockwise and counter-clockwise spin, dependent upon which hempishere you reside in and this spin creates a giant magnet.

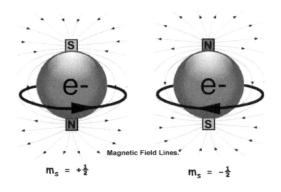

(*Magnetic Field Lines*)

My initial spiritual awakening involved time travel, 159 years back in time to Victorian England. I stepped into another time event and was taken to the scene of a crime moments before it happened (again). This was recorded in my e-book 'When Murder Travels Through Time'. Past present and future are all happening at the same time in snapshots which create a continuous time line. Time is also the way in which we can measure both speed and distance. I believe that I was able to remote view by time reversal symmetry and time reversal symmetry is where physics works the same forwards as it does backwards. Particles, which also form consciousness entanglement, know their direction of travel because the route going forward in time is different to the route coming back in time and they can sense the difference and know their direction of travel. Entanglement is where pairs of particles (minute matter) physically interact. 'Remote Viewing' is consciousness entanglement where there is a targeted interaction between viewer and target, regardless of the distance between them and it deals with information as processed by consciousness. Remote viewing is the application of consciousness that permits a person-viewer to give details (past-present-future) about something normally inaccessible to normal senses due to time etc.

The 'Princeton Engineering Anomalies Research' (PEAR) proved that remote viewing can be replicated in controlled conditions and the experimental data supported a 'backward in time signalling'. Particles are matter and matter is conscious and matter as consciousness is known as perceptronium. Thoughts are energy and energy is matter and therefore thoughts become matter which is manifestation. My particle consciousness (conscious entanglement) was able to go back and remote view an event that had already happened in my time, because it was still happening elsewhere in another time event. What is the light at the end of the tunnel? People who have had a Near Death Experience (NDE) speak of it when they return from the grip of mortality.

The light at the end of the tunnel is an electromagnetic flux pointer to a higher dimension of 'Hyperspace', hyperspace meaning beyond three dimensions. It is a projection of our own Zero-Point-Energy (ZPE) that continues to live (our own real-self)

It is a tunnel of singularity and singularity is the point of an object that is mathematically undefined. I would make comment that this is the nodal point that Nikola Tesla referred to which is a portal from the third dimension to the fourth and this is also how the soul/spirit enters the body and resides in the mind. At ZPE motion ceases and molecules come to rest. At the speed of light time is frozen and space is contracted to zero. Light travels in a straight line but if it is curved then it slows down and therefore within the speed of light there is no time but there is ZPE. Photons within the body and outside the body travel at the speed of light. Biophotons are emitted by the body and can be released through mental intention. They may also modulate fundamental processes within cell to cell communication and DNA. DNA and cells use biophotons to store and communicate information. Human body photons are ultra weak photon emissions (UPE) with visibility a 1000 times lower than we can see with the naked eye. Therefore time travel is occurring within the body also and biophotons are messanger particles. This is symbolised by the halo, which is the illumination of the mind.

A zero Point Field is the lowest energy state, a ground state, where molecules come to rest and motion ceases and a field in physics is a physical quantity.

When our essence leaves the physical body, it is leaving the mechanisms of the brain, where it resides, and our consciousness particles (consciousness entanglement) travels down the tunnel of singularity and back to hyperspace, taking the appearance of a tunnel of light,the gateway between here and there. The zero point energy centers around the consciousness that continues into the hyperspace beyond the nearest black hole tunnel of singularity. The quantum vacuum in the hyperspace provides the pleasant experience in near death experience by enabling the quantum level of the zero point energy to leap into a higher level. There are also miniature blackholes within the brain and DNA called 'Vacuum Domains'

It is a quantum level projection of the energy transformation from one level to another level. The transformation requires a complete transformation of spatial dimension from our universe's 3D to higher dimensions of the hyperspace. This requires systematic unbundling of energy quanta in a retrograde flow of time and space. That also explains the play back of the whole life in near death experience that some people have, similar to a life-review. I would make comment that this is the nodal point that Nikola Tesla referred to which is a portal from the third dimension to the fourth and this is also how the soul/spirit enters the body and resides in the mind. When our essence leaves the physical body, it is leaving the mechanisms of the brain, where it resides, and our consciousness particles (consciousness entanglement) travels down the tunnel of singularity and back to hyperspace, taking the appearance of a tunnel of light, the gateway between here and there. The zero point energy centers around the consciousness that continues into the hyperspace beyond the nearest black hole tunnel of singularity. The quantum vacuum in the hyperspace provides the pleasant experience in near death experience by enabling the quantum level of the zero point energy to leap into a higher level. There are also miniature blackholes within the brain and DNA called 'Vacuum Domains'

It is a quantum level projection of the energy transformation from one level to another level. The transformation requires a complete transformation of spatial dimension from our universe's 3D to higher dimensions of the hyperspace. This requires systematic un-bundling of energy quanta in a retrograde flow of time and space. That also explains the play back of the whole life in near death experience that some people have, similar to a life-review At ZPE motion ceases and molecules come to rest. At the speed of light time is frozen and space is contracted to zero. Light travels in a straight line but if it is curved then it slows down and therefore within the speed of light there is no time but there is ZPE. Photons within the body and outside the body travel at the speed of light. Biophotons are emitted by the body and can be released through mental intention. They may also modulate fundamental processes within cell to cell communication and DNA. DNA and cells use biophotons to store and communicate information. Human body photons are ultra weak photon emissions (UPE) with visibility a 1000 times lower than we can see with the naked eye. Therefore time travel is occurring within the body also and biophotons are messanger particles. This is symbolised by the halo, which is the illumination of the mind.

Time Continued:

Even nature, namely the fertilisation event, is timed to mathematical certainty.

After fertilisation, the cells in the zygote divide rapidly to form a morula, which becomes the embryo after approximately five days. The fetus is present about eight weeks after the fertilisation takes place. After fertilisation, the zygote begins to divide rapidly. Twenty-four hours after fertilisation, the zygote contains two cells, and three days after fertilisation, the zygote has 16 cells and is called a morula. The cells continue to divide and form a hollow bundle called a blastocyst. The blastocyst implants in the endometrium, and the cells begin to form the embryo.

The embryo is present at five to six days after the zygote is fertilised. The embryo is a clump of cells inside the formerly hollow blastocyst, and is surrounded by the trophoblast. The trophoblast contains cells that direct hormone production and implantation.

After the embryo forms, the cells form the embryonic disk. The embryonic disk begins to fold, allowing the cells within the disk to touch other cells.

The cells then start forming each of the bodily systems. For example, the organs and nervous system begin to develop at this stage. After approximately three weeks, each of the cells in the developing embryo are part of one of the developing systems in the body. After eight weeks, the embryo becomes a fetus.

This is programmed time. Genetics are timed to activate at certain points and this is time as we know it. It is time and mathematics as one, set to activate after a certain duration has passed!

And since atoms are 99.9999999999999% empty space, we can see a time-space continuum within our genetic code.

Time truly exists and, as the universe is mathematical, both are intrinsically linked and inseparable.

Light takes 8 minutes to reach Earth from the Sun, the Earth takes 365 days to orbit the Sun, Mars 687 Earth days, Venus 224 Earth days, and so on. From the time a star is born to the time it explodes and dies is time. Man is locked into a chrono-biology, which is biological time with Earth's night and day cycles.

It is all timed! We are locked into a concept called time, a duration of events or the intervals between them which we use to quantify rates of change of quantities in material reality or in the conscious experience. Time is often referred to as a fourth dimension along with three spatial dimensions. As a third dimensional creation, we skip from one block of third dimensional time to another which, in order to continue to function as dimensionality, must have a definitive separation which is our life and death cycle. It's the transition from linear to lateral time, a change of viewpoint as the movie slides that are our life flicker from one scene to the next. Everything has a place and everything is a part of everything else and there is no separation. Even in what we consider to be empty space is really full, there is only the result of limited sight and frequency bandwidth through a frequency filter. The universe is panpsychism, where everything has a consciousness.

These are just a few of many such examples.

For as long as the universe continues to expand, time will continue to exist. And if there was to be another universal Big Bang, then we would be part of another timeline. DNA is atomic, and therefore DNA responds to time.

An atom is the smallest particle of a chemical element that can exist.

The same Russian scientists mentioned earlier are now saying that DNA follows the same rules as all of our human languages. To this end, they compared the rules of syntax (the way in which words are put together to form phrases and sentences), semantics (the study of meaning in language forms), and the basic rules of grammar. DNA is arranged in such a precise way that it reveals a set of arithmetic patterns and ideographic symbolic language. This is the basis of Egyptian hieroglyphs and even the Nazca Line land patterns, both are a pictogram language, also known as a ideogram or ideograph. Ancient languages used sacred geometry hidden inside the language where the sounds of words carry enormous power and can be decoded using numbers. It is a mathematical expression written as words.

Human beings are a three billion letter code, and this figure doesn't include the dormant DNA (what science wrongly calls junk DNA) which is yet to be activated. Time can, of course, be manipulated by such things as time dilation and, as you approach a black hole of space, time slows down as black holes emit a frequency of 460 hertz, which slows down time and can change brain wave states.

In which case, and on that basis, we should be able to reverse aging within our mind and body.

Within our DNA, we also have black holes called 'vacuum domains'. The black holes of the brain are connected to the black holes of space (planetophysical physics). 460 hertz are isochronic tones, which are brainwave entrainment and they are an audio-based way to stimulate your brainwave activity. A vacuum is a space devoid of matter but in the likes of the Casimir effect which is vacuum energy fom empty space, it can exert a force upon physical objects.

They can guide your dominant brainwave activity to a different frequency, changing your mental state into a meditative state. In DNA, vacuum domains can cause patterns in the vacuum, producing magnetised wormholes which are microscopic equivalents of universal wormholes. There are tunnel connections between entirely different areas in the universe, through which information can be transmitted outside of space and time. The DNA attracts these bits of information and passes them onto our consciousness, and this is a form of hyper-communication.

Vacuum domains are self-radiant balls of light or ionised gas that occur when an electron separates from its parent atom. This can be guided by thought, and can react to thought as the wavelengths are similar. They are luminous effects created by combined forces of electromagnetics and gravitational principles that can manifest localised mini black holes of gravispin, creating a vacuum effect and a pulsed heat release. These balls of light have been seen creating crop circles, and crop circles contain diatonic ratios which are an intelligent communication through sound; it may even be a message hidden within soundwaves. The balls of light that have been recorded creating crop circles have also been recorded as having intelligence communication between one another.

(Group-focused Consciousness can create vacuum domains)

Zulus call crop circles 'Izishoze Zamatongo', which means 'writings of the Gods', and they were first recorded in Europe in 1590, although in some parts of the world earlier than that.

This, of course, could then lead us onto the biblical word, where everything was spoken into existence. If language is a reflection of our inherent DNA, then that, too, was spoken into existence, through the power of manifestation. We, as Gods, must also then have that capability, and this is called the 'Law of Attraction', a universal creative power detailed in the book of St. Thomas which was removed from the Bible by agents of the Church. Why, does someone not want us to have this knowledge?

TWO

POLICE ENCOUNTERS OF THE THIRD KIND

I am mentioning several of my own personal encounters (although there are many more) because I mention ETs throughout the book and, in doing so, I feel that it is important to have at least personally experienced them. I have seen many speakers held in high esteem on the global circuit who haven't ever seen anything remotely extra-terrestrial, not even once!

I have seen, and have had, many experiences of the supernatural kind and personally know that we have visitors here to our planet that may not have originated from here or they may even have always been here, it's difficult to say. Regardless of whichever that is, they are here in our skies and not in a galaxy far, far away. What you are about to read is a small insight into my unusual life that has been so very different to that of the average person. I was a frontline police officer in the UK for 17 years and I saw both many earthly things and unearthly things that have no orthodox explanation. I was often out at times that many people were not and, as such, I had sight of places that many don't see, when activities would occur in dark and desolate areas. I am a trained investigator and expert witness in court, and thus evidence gathering was second nature to me. I eliminated all possibilities before any conclusion was ever reached. So why have I experienced so much? "You are meant for this work. First you had to be part of it to know what you were learning about to help others" (Galactic channelling). This is why!

I hope that you enjoy sharing, through my eyes, the things that I have been privileged to see.

ENCOUNTER #1: The Night They Came To Visit – The Landing Site

"I happen to have been privileged enough to be in on the fact that we've been visited on this planet and the UFO phenomena is real"
- Dr Edgar Mitchell (Astronaut)

A night filled of dark matter, sporting pockets of eternal light above us, but it was clear and unusually charged like the jousting lance of a brave knight on the back of his loyal stallion. This was to be an unorthodox evening to rival any other that had manifested before it. Parade over, I boarded my police vehicle with Sarah, my wife, as passenger, for a night shift with a difference. "Mobile 30, can you make an intruder alarm?" The radio crackled and the controller's voice came through giving the location. On my way, not too far away, but what will I find there, is it a genuine alarm call, or is it just a regular false alarm? First to arrive; but nothing amiss at ground level, at least. With other officers present, we looked to the sky. A flash of light caused by two juxtaposed shooting stars travelling faster than the blink of my eyes, but these were not shooting stars, as their odyssey turned them into warped luminescent dots, a scene from *Star Trek* in my vicinity and not my TV screen. An eerie feeling hung around the air. We are not in control tonight, there is something much bigger in town, a presence that gave us the shivers. "Mobile 30, can you attend intruders in a rear garden?" The radio crackles again, the same area, and we're on our way. As street lights turn off, we arrive again; no-one in the garden at all, but the caller is adamant, figures have been seen in the garden walking around. One final look and nothing in sight, we leave, but as we reached the street outside the callers house, another call comes through from the same person, the intruders are back! But there was nothing again. Impossible for an escape as we were already there, just feet away. Other calls of an exact nature are now coming in, in the area, but too far away for it to be the same people. The exact same scenario, intruders in the garden, officers arrive, no-one there, they leave, and further calls are received to say the intruders/silhouettes are back. Now streets lights are turning off, the whole area spanning for miles is pitch black, the sounds of explosions caused by electrical charges are heard all around us, one after the other, like bombs activating. Then, the most deafening of sounds. A manhole cover is blown out of the road as its circular metal cover, reminiscent of a UFO disc itself, flies through the air but lands safely a short distance away. Now the atmosphere can be cut by a knife; we are definitely not in control here.

Inner senses are stirring like a whirlwind, detecting outsider presences as my energy field meets the dimensionally invisible, but my radar has made contact. The electricity board confirmed that they had had 9 underground sub-station explosions that evening, which is totally out of the ordinary as they usually expect one, if that! An evening of call after call, incident after incident, with nothing to show for it other than the scene from a disaster movie. Shift over, it's 7am, and we're on our way home, arriving soon after. Sitting at our laptop, we contact a local UFO group by email who, because of our regular sightings, we had spoken to several times before. We detail all that had happened that night but, as we did so, our emails disappeared from their folder only to be returned several minutes later, like they had been removed, copied, and then put back, as we witnessed each stage of this process. We had experienced things like this before with the bugging of our landline and mobile phones as they began to tap, activated by certain keywords during personal conversations, which was confirmed by a phone engineer who found a strange device in the main telephone wire box outside our house. GCHQ were a likely culprit. The UFO group also investigated and spoke with the electricity board, who confirmed the same information to them. Take your mind back to the 80s movie *ET*; the landing, the crew disembarking their craft and scurrying around the area on that starlit night. What if that location had been densely populated? Just think how many calls the local police would have received that night about intruders in the garden and following unusual activity in the skies. I no longer have to think as I look back on my former career; I have been amongst it and there is a power greater than we know just a micron away, not in a galaxy far, far away, but a mere frequency outside of our own.

ENCOUNTER #2: When In Rome

Although Sarah and I have had lots of UFO experiences, our first actual sighting was whilst on holiday in central Rome, quite close to the Colosseum back in 2007. It was around 6.30pm and we were out walking and observing the wonderful sights, looking from open grassy areas between buildings. Sarah began to look with interest in a particular area of sky and so, naturally, I also looked in that direction. We both then saw a light grey oval-shaped cloud in the distance that was moving slowly to our left along with other clouds, but this was no usual cloud. It was different, darker, and more rounded in its shape. As we observed it, it moved towards our right-hand side in the opposite direction to where the other clouds were now going, ruling out any wind propulsion, and was going against nature's direction. As we continued to watch, the cloud changed shape into a spiral, like a vortex or tornado, becoming darker as if it was becoming more solid, probably as a result of a frequency change. Matter becomes dense when it slows down and that's when it is visible in our frequency spectra; as humans, we see less than 1% of what is out there, as a lot is going on in the invisible 99% that we only sometimes catch a glimpse of. The object now appeared to fade in and out. After about 30 seconds, the object split into two spheres that were now flying separately, yet close to each other. They were darting around the sky as if under some sort of intelligent control, but in unison, synchronised swimming in the sky, a practised routine. The object then, again, joined as one before separating for a second time to

28

become two individual shapes again, like an air show display. It then disappeared from sight and we never saw the object again. All in all, the incident lasted several minutes, but no-one else seemed to notice the occurrence.

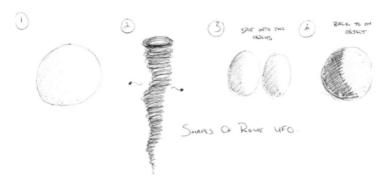

(Sketch of the Object)

The conversation afterwards far outlived the time of the incident itself. It was to be our first of many encounters of this kind. Once we joined together as a unit, unusual things began to happen with intense frequency, sometimes even daily. To infinity and beyond!

ENCOUNTER #3: Cigar Or No Cigar!

Another sighting for us was in broad daylight on a bright and sunny afternoon in our hometown. We were driving through the town, negotiating several mini-islands and avoiding heavy traffic. The day and location was nothing unusual at that point, and it was a journey that we had undertaken hundreds of times before without incident. Sarah and I looked up into the sky and both saw three large cigar-shaped metallic crafts about 300 feet above us, positioned close to each other and at the same height, but in different areas of the sky. They were stationary, suspended in mid-air, and were completely silent. The crafts themselves had no visible markings and seemed smooth metal, without hideous rivets or alike.

After several seconds, in essence just a brief glimpse, the objects just seemed to vanish. However, they would have been in the same place; we had just drifted out of their frequency level and therefore lost sight of them through vibrational invisibility. These crafts use what is known as 'Magnetic Space Propulsion', which is riding on the crest of the waves of electrical currents that are present in the sky and the wider electromagnetic universe as a means of travel. The two best known shapes for this traverse are the disc and the cigar/tubular/cylindrical shapes. And people often wonder why UFOs are usually one of these shapes. Their rapid speed is aided by single magnetic polarity. It's a shame we couldn't see within the structure to wave at the pilots, whoever they were.

ENCOUNTER #4: The Openings of Dimensional Gateways

There have been two occasions where Sarah and I have been witness to the opening of dimensional gateways/doorways in our reality. Just as we would open a door to venture from one room to another within our house, there are those with advanced knowledge of physics who can do the same within the universe and drift in and out of dimensions. As the Jesuit biblical quote once stated, "My father's house has many rooms" John 14:2, this is really talking about the dimensional make-up of the universe. The Bible is full of hidden meanings of a similar nature that get missed by superficial stories. The first experience we had with gateways was one evening on a night shift, when Sarah and I were in the same police vehicle. We were on general patrol on a clear night around midnight. As we both looked up into the sky, we saw a beautiful, glowing, light blue, teardrop shape which just appeared in the sky. As we observed the shape, the end appeared to open up and emit another smaller object that came out of it and again into the sky. It looked as if the initial object had given birth to the smaller one but, in reality, it had travelled through the opening and into our reality. The smaller object continued to travel as it left the teardrop and disappeared a short distance along the sky, as did the original gateway; it just simply faded away out of sight, leaving the night sky as it once was just prior to the event, never to be seen by us again. We were trained observers, trained to gather evidence with a keen eye, we were not easily fooled, and we did not easily jump to conclusions, but we eliminated all possibilities bar the reality of the situation. The second occasion was similar, however, this was in a park at night at ground level; a sort of personal Rendlesham Forest event. Sarah, I, and a friend were out walking in nature as we did frequently, so we knew the area very well, despite it being a dark place at night with very little street lighting amid thick forestry. As we walked through parkland and looked ahead, trying to see a route in which to travel, a safe direction due to the lack of light, we all saw a magnificent pure white light, so bright it hurt our eyes to look directly into it, appear at ground level about 20 feet in front of us. It covered that immediate area and was seemingly circling trees and grassy areas like a luminous smoke. Sarah's mobile phone camera, which she had been holding, went off by itself, and below is the image caught. It appeared white to the naked eye but there were many colours that we couldn't see that were picked up on film. This made for an interesting conversation at the end of the evening.

ENCOUNTER #5: The Orange Craft, One of Our Five A Day

Again, it was a night shift however , on this occasion, Sarah and I were in different vehicles but in the same vicinity. It was a lovely glistening night covered by stars. I had just finished dealing with an incident and was standing on the doorstep of a house with a police colleague and two paramedics, waiting to leave the area. When I looked up at the sky, I saw a large but bright orange orb of light above us in the sky itself, about 200 feet high. It was also seen by the other officer and the paramedics; one of whom said, "What's that?" It was moving faster than an airplane but seemed about the same size as a small aircraft. I initially thought that it was a plane in distress, a possible engine fire, as the orb appeared like a fireball and I was close to calling the incident in to make local air traffic control aware. It was also an orange orb that had followed the police helicopter on one occasion back towards the airport, whereby permission to approach the airport had been denied because of its presence. The police logs were quickly restricted so that no-one could view the details, and it was also recorded by on-board helicopter cameras. The orange orb moved in a circular path past us and, after a couple of minutes, it disappeared from sight. I called Sarah to tell her all about it, very disappointed that she hadn't seen it, although she was in the same area anyway. Since the orb had now gone, or so I believed, I left the area to go to another incident elsewhere. To my surprise, Sarah called me stating that the object was back in the same location that I had seen it in. This was the second circuit, as if putting on another show. Was this deliberate? We may never know, but on the occasion that I had seen something without her, she still got to see the show!

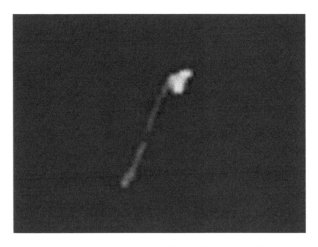

(Actual picture taken by Sarah of the Orange Orb in question, which looked completely different with the naked eye, it was a ball of fire. Picture 2, another of our UFO encounters from another incident) yet another strange encounter for us, there seems to be a pattern emerging here!)

ENCOUNTER #6: Flight of the Navigator

Growing up in the 80's meant being in the best decade for film and music, a widely agreed upon fact. One of those movies was called *Flight of the Navigator* by Steven Spielberg, who had a fascination with extra-terrestrial themes. But why do we mention this particular movie? It just so happens that the craft in that film bears a striking resemblance to a small craft that we saw in the UK Channel Islands, St Helier in Jersey to be exact. In fact, we would say that it was an unmanned probe of similar size to the Foo Fighters witnessed by WWII bomber pilots that followed their planes, even possibly the same craft. Again, it was broad daylight and we were walking along the promenade next to the sandy beach. The area was fairly quiet that day, apart from light traffic on the nearby main road. As we looked above us, which at that time in our life we did due to the constant events we were experiencing, we saw a small teardrop-shaped craft, completely flying silently above us, going out towards the ocean.

(Not our photo but similar to what we saw - picture is from *Flight of the Navigator* movie) It blended in very well with the colour of its surroundings and just floated/flew in a remote-controlled fashion until we lost sight of it as it went further and further out to sea, like a chameleon gradually becoming unseen. Does Spielberg know more than he is letting on? We bet that he does!

ENCOUNTER #7: A Scene From *Close Encounters,* The Movie

Another great 80's Spielberg film about extra-terrestrial visitation. The main characters were plagued by feelings, sensations, and visions that they couldn't initially explain, but it was driving them to the point of insanity. A mountain that they had seen and carved out of mash potato and alike, until they saw the location on TV and knew that this was the message, they needed to go to that location at a certain time and certain day, an invite. But can this happen? Is there any element of truth in this possibility? Yes there is and, by now, you won't be surprised to know that it happened to me, Sarah, and a couple of friends. The scenario was this. About an hour's drive away from our house there is a location called the Clent Hills, which house a set of ancient monoliths at the top of the hills themselves at the summit. The previous night, I kept getting a strong 'gut feeling' that I needed to attend the place and go to these hills, in fact, a very strong feeling. I was also shown images of orbs floating towards me from all directions of the landscape as they came to the summit and stone monoliths; it was a clear image. Some of the group also had the feeling that they needed to go, although the images seemed to be for me. The next evening, we all arrived and stood by the monoliths on top of the hill, which gave us a clear view for miles, albeit at night. I, or we, couldn't see anything happening with the naked eye but could sense a large object above us in the sky. At the same time, all four of us had a feeling that we needed to rotate from one monolith to the other until we finished where we had started. This was in anti/counter-clockwise motion which is a positive movement, ironically, there were four monoliths and four of us so, effectively, one each to stand next to. After the evening had finished and we looked back at the pictures we had taken of what was seemingly the street lights from the hill, we saw orbs floating towards us from all directions, exactly as I had seen it in my visions the previous night! We don't know what had happened that night or what we had been involved in, but it was something significant in our view. We may never find out.

(Actual picture from the Clent Hills)

ENCOUNTER #8: They Walk Amongst Us

Earth's history is littered with recorded images and documented meetings with beings from another world or another time and place. It was such meetings that were meant to have resulted in influential civilisations such as the Egyptians, Babylonians, and Sumerians, etc. receiving advanced mathematical sequences and codes that enabled them to build such monuments as the pyramids, which I have briefly touched on as being part of a universal pyramid matrix system and not a solitary idea like we are led to believe. We can prove that by way of mathematical codes which even direct us to the planet Mars and the Cydonian city (face and pyramids) that they themselves direct us back to the likes of Stonehenge and Giza in Egypt with their mathematical coordinates. Many people have reported seeing, speaking to, and have even claimed to be contacts for extra-terrestrial groups. I often wondered how valid a claim this was, based on it being a trust rather than evidence as only they truly know what they saw. I did believe that it was possible; after all, we had seen so many of them in our skies that we knew they were here. However, it took a further twist one day when we attended an event in a nearby city about multidimensionality, UFOs, and beings from other places! We had been at the event for a few hours. Sarah describes the encounter from this point on… "We were sitting down for a bite to eat in the foyer area just by the double doors into the main event and doors to outside. Mick had just popped out to the shop across the street, leaving me and a friend at the table. Suddenly, outside, a dog that was chained up began barking intently as if in distress. As we sat there, a strange looking, what can only be described as a 'person', loosely speaking, walked in. As he entered the foyer, he stopped still, arms and hands poised as if he was just about to draw a revolver. He was about 6'3 – 6'4" tall, wearing a dark three-quarter length coat jacket with shoulder pads, and old suit trousers with a pair of old grey pumps. He had a stretched and taut skin, pale white, and what looked like greying blonde shoulder length hair that could have been hundreds of years old, brittle-looking, as if it would have crumbled if touched. It was brushed back from the forehead. We were hit by a very uncomfortable energy. His face was like no 'human' face I'd ever seen before. He had the strangest look with his mouth wide open as if stuck. It didn't close. He stood there silently, slowly looking from left to right as if scanning the area inside. Twice he looked directly at me and, astonishingly, I noticed his eyes didn't seem to have any whites to them, appearing glassy and dark grey with no apparent irises. Quite frankly, he was scary! The area wasn't busy, with a maximum of 8 or 9 people in the vicinity. He was around 7 feet away from me and my view was unobstructed.

He continued to look left and right and took a step or two forwards before stopping and looking slowly left and right again, his mouth still gaping open but no words spoken. He took another step towards the double doors to the main event and stopped in front of it. He slowly reached out an arm and opened the doors, advancing another couple of steps and eventually moving through to the event, standing next to, ironically, a man that had earlier given a talk about being abducted. I said to the friend that was with us "He's not human!" and I meant it. She replied, "I know". At this point, Michael returned and, as he walked in, we pointed in the man's direction inside the room. Michael took one look at the man and came back gobsmacked. Mick and I had to leave at that point, but our friend who was present with us remained at the event and returned inside where the 'man' had gone. She text shortly afterwards to say that he was now nowhere to be seen, as if he had vanished into thin air. Upon looking further into it, his features seemed to fit into the category of 'Tall White' ET... But who knows?

(Left – Sarah's sketch of what she saw, Right – A friend's sketch of the same 'being')

There have, of course, been more incidents that we could have recited but, for now, we hope that this has given you an insight into our lives, a life much different to many others. Why us, and where it's going is a question we cannot at this point in time answer for you; something happened when Sarah and I met and started a relationship and subsequently married, something extraordinary.

There are those who have awareness of world events and beyond. There are many wheels within wheels in the truth movements who have formed the spokes for their own wheels, disregarding the other three that elevate the car. They have their own set of beliefs and a belief system that takes them away from the mainstream, but simply from one branch of the tree to another one; usually the next one in line and not that much further. New battle lines are drawn and the world sees a new army to take on the fight for justice and disclosure, but that fight is often the wrong one as truth groups then pit against each other as the real culprits who start the wars, sit back and laugh at the schism they have steered from the same offices and halls of power that gave us the divisive religious system of control many thousands of years ago in order to divide us. I have been to many conferences and events run by UFO groups who spend a lifetime waiting to see an object in the sky, that tin can that they can call a UFO sighting. Waiting patiently at the station for the end of that long universal journey made to Earth; through cosmic spaces and galactic gateways. But what's behind the UFO and why does the interest of many end there? It is more than just a tin can. It seems that the ceiling has many levels, but far too many are happy to stop at the fabricated and capped ceiling and not look beyond the tiles themselves. Planet Earth has always had visitations; it has always had visitors who have been an integral part of humanity and our temporary place of residence. We see it in ancient documentations and we can see it in many of the famous monuments that the local population of the time claimed to have been given information for by a strange group of non-humans who gave them mathematical numbers that they used in their monuments. We can see it when we look at monuments on other planets, such as Mars, that give coordinates of Earth monuments such as Stonehenge and the Pyramids of Egypt, and vice versa it has to be said, a mathematical matrix system of encoded numbers. This can only happen with interplanetary contact and co-operation of wider quantums. We have seen cigar-shaped crafts during the day above us. We have seen dimensional gateways open up at night with crafts emerging into the night sky, and we have been involved in what was possibly a landing of some kind that electrified the area into an eerie atmosphere and feeling of 'we're not in control here'! We as humans can only see less than 1% of the frequency spectra, so what is operating within the 99% that we cannot see?

Amongst a universe that is not empty but is in fact full and teaming with life, there exists a community that we have shut off from. We are part of a galactic society of multiple realities and dimensions that we can travel in and out of yet, for some reason, we choose to look at things from a minute prospective and not a universal one. When we open up our ceilings and look beyond our own box of tricks, we will open ourselves up to a much wider reality and, at that point, we will see more of what there is to see. In-fighting amongst the righteous and sword bearers of society will get the warriors of truth nowhere at all, only to a level one of infinity, which is where they'll stay. Keep your feet firmly on common ground and don't deviate into egotistical rivalry; that will nullify any good cause. Multi-dimensional and intergalactic beings exist, they are here, they always have been, they never left, and they walk openly amongst us.

THREE

THE ANUNNAKI:
A METAPHOR FOR THE HIGHER HUMAN

To challenge Zecharia Sitchen and the Anunnaki is like challenging Christ at a church or religious convention, and I happily do both!

The fact remains that if there is evidence to challenge a story, and in most cases that's exactly what they are, then that should be presented to others. Why shouldn't a lie or a misunderstanding of the real meaning not be exposed, or at least questioned?

The Anunnaki story has become the shrine of many UFO groups who fight you with unsavoury language should you not subscribe to its version of history. But, for me, I see a different version of the Sumerian scrolls than the version translated by Sitchen, a self-taught reader of Cuneiform. I would never deny the existence of ETs, as I have personally seen and stood next to one. I have personally seen a multitude of UFOs; many of which you would have read about in an earlier chapter and, as a direct result of what I have seen, I have been monitored by GCHQ here in the UK, I have had my phones tapped and my emails removed, copied, and returned. Something is clearly going on!

I have studied all the famous ancient cultures of Earth, their monuments and their sacred religious scriptures, and I have found a code, a code that is really telling us about ourselves, our own enlightenment, and our own consciousness through the genetic workings of the human body. This is the real purpose of these wonderful monumental structures that are acting as giant replicas of inner processes and an amplification of the inner rituals that achieve them.

I see the same message within the Sumerian scrolls, namely a message of human genetics, geometric metaphors, and consciousness. The Sitchen version tells us that a race of ETs known as the Anunnaki, meaning those who from Heaven to Earth came, visited Earth on their home planet Nibiru (Planet X) which is now in a 3600 year Earth orbit, to mine for Gold which was needed to rectify the dwindling atmosphere on their planet. They supposedly used the genetics of Homo-erectus to create a slave race (Lulu) that we know of today as Homo-sapiens, our current human form. Their principle characters were Anu, Alalu, Enki, and Enlil, amongst others. But I am going to tell you my version of the story, which completely matches the message of all other ancient cultures of the time. You are about to read an alternative view, an unpopular view amongst many groups. But, nevertheless, I am confident that I am right in what I say, and I am also confident that one day my findings will be verified as being correct.

I now invite you to the ancient land of Sumer.

The Anunnaki are a group of deities that appear in the mythological traditions of the ancient Sumerians, Akkadians, Assyrians, and Babylonians.

Descriptions of how many Anunnaki there actually were and what role they fulfilled are inconsistent and often contradictory. In the earliest Sumerian writings about them, which come from the Post-Akkadian period, the Anunnaki are the most powerful deities in the pantheon, descendants of Anu, the God of the Heavens, and their primary function is to decree the fates of humanity.

The Anunnaki are a group of deities in ancient Mesopotamian cultures. The name is variously written "a-nuna", "a-nuna-ke-ne", or "a-nun-na", meaning something to the effect of "those of royal blood" or "princely offspring". A widespread etymology is that the name derived from the union of Heaven with the Earth. Their relation to the group of Gods known as the Igigi is unclear to the mainstream but clear to me and, at times, the names are used synonymously. But in the Atra-Hasis flood myth, the Igigi are the sixth generation of the Gods who have to work for the Anunnaki, rebelling after 40 days and replaced by the creation of humans.

Jeremy Black and Anthony Green offer a slightly different perspective on the Igigi and the Anunnaki, writing that "Igigu or Igigi is a term introduced in the Old Babylonian Period as a name for the "great gods"." While it sometimes kept that sense in later periods, from Middle Assyrian and Babylonian times on it is generally used to refer to the Gods of Heaven collectively, just as the term 'Anunnaki' was later used to refer to the Gods of the Underworld. In the Epic of Creation, it is said that there are 300 Igigu of Heaven.

It is stated by Zecharia Sitchen that this group of extra-terrestrials came to Earth upon their planet Nibiru, which is now stuck in a 3600 year orbit around Earth, to mine for gold to repair the dwindling atmosphere of their own planet. When they arrived, they found life and eventually tinkered with its DNA to create what we have today, the modern human Homo-sapiens, as a slave race to mine for gold for them.

There were many chief Gods such as Anu, Enlil, Ninlil, Enki, Alalu, and others.

There were struggles between the various Gods; Enlil wanted to keep this new slave race in ignorance of truth and Enki wanted to pass sacred knowledge onto them. Ninlil asked the Council of Seven to create Eridu (the biblical Eden) for Adamu and Tiamat to live.

Alalu was the supervisor of the gold mining expedition but, after a fight with Anu, he was banished to planet Mars where he died and the face on Mars was built as his tomb as a commemoration.

But is there a different version of history, a version that fits in with the whole teachings of the ancient world? Could it be that the story is, in fact, just a grand metaphor for something else?

Yes it can, and yes it is, as you will soon see!

The late author Zecharia Sitchen, in my opinion, as have numerous universities around the world, made a literal translation of the famous Sumerian scrolls. I acknowledge his arduous work and I am not in any way tarnishing his memory or his opinions and beliefs.

I would even go as far as to say that some of them were here on this planet before humans and that we are actually visiting them! This would account for various advanced civilisations finding many of the famous monuments of the world already built.

The Egyptians, for example, who documented everything that they did, made no official record of themselves building the pyramids. This seems a little strange, to say the least. The pyramids are monuments of great pride and deep knowledge, and you would shout it from the highest peak if you were the architects and builders of such a wonder of the world.

But I have a different version of the whole Anunnaki story and the Sumerian scrolls, based on several years of researching Earth's ancient cultures and their often secret encrypted messages within their monuments and even biblical scripture. 2019 makes my tenth year as an esoteric researcher following my 17 years of being a police investigator. 27 years of my life have been digging deep and finding the connections that are there left for us to find.

It is a code that I call the ancient code and it connects all of the ancient cultures together in a way denied and misunderstood by modern scholars. There is sufficient evidence to prove an ancient global connection. They had access to the same advanced knowledge base which has been ciphered into their monuments. I have found and deciphered that knowledge base. But when something has been misinterpreted, deliberately or not, it remains untrue, and much of our history has been misinterpreted.

ZECHARIA SITCHEN: HIS - STORY (History)

Zecharia Sitchen was born on 11th July 1920 in Azerbaijan. He obtained a degree at the London School of Economics. He became a journalist in mandatory Palestine (Israel) before working for a shipping company in New York. It was at this point in his life that he taught himself cuneiform.

Cuneiform, or Sumerian cuneiform, one of the earliest systems of writing, was invented by the Sumerians. It is distinguished by its wedge-shaped marks on clay tablets, made by means of a blunt reed for a stylus. The name 'cuneiform' itself simply means "wedge-shaped".

Sumer is the region where the modern day Iraq is now situated.

It has been suggested that he was a CIA disinformation agent and that he had connections to the Vatican Church. I have written extensively in other literature about the Vatican Church and its control of the world population through various infiltrated sects and cults. Sitchen wrote numerous bestselling books on this subject and travelled to various countries around the world. Ironically, many of his Anunnaki books are classified as 'fiction'.

He died on 9th October 2010 but was an author of books proposing an explanation for human origins involving ancient astronauts. Sitchin attributed the creation of the ancient Sumerian culture to the Anunnaki, which he stated was a race of extra-terrestrials from a planet beyond Neptune called Nibiru.

He asserted that Sumerian mythology suggests that this hypothetical planet of Nibiru is in an elongated 3600-year-long elliptical orbit around the solar Sun. Sitchin's books have sold millions of copies worldwide and have been translated into more than 25 languages. 3600 gives us 3+6+0+0=9.

I will soon introduce you to my explanation of this famous story and it is not what you may think!

My personal take is that many races we regard as ETs were actually here before humans and are the true original inhabitants of this planet, although not all, which would fit in perfectly with the viewpoint that the likes of the Egyptians did not build the pyramids and found them already there.

What these ancient monuments did and were constructed for was a ritualistic changing of brain waves and an altered state of the mind and consciousness. This can be seen with the mathematical number sequences that form the basis of these famous structures, mathematical sequences that hold a consciousness raising frequency, such as the Golden ratio, the Fibonacci sequence and, of course, PI.

These monuments were not built for optical pleasure for tourists many thousands of years in the future, they were built as power stations to enhance consciousness processes for the initiates of the time.

To me, the creator of all things is a pure mathematical mind, a geometer, and is indeed the divine shape the circle, whose centre is everywhere and whose circumference is nowhere. Infinity can be divided within the circle. This is shown in the Temple of Osiris in Egypt with the flower of life that has been burnt onto the wall.

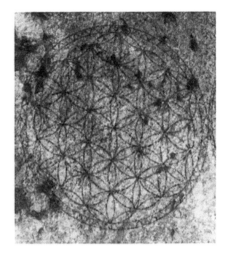

(Temple of Abydos)

The circle is infinite spirit and spirit is the non-decaying spin of the electron which then leads us into atoms and their three sub-atomic particles. It is quite apparent to anyone who possesses a thinking mind that we are not the only life form in the universe, the solar system, or even planet Earth, and how could we be?

I have personally seen too much for me to think otherwise.

But what if these intricate shapes on the sacred landscapes are a message? There is always the argument that crop circles are man-made and, undoubtedly, some are just that, but how do you then explain the 'Mandelbrot Set' crop circle? The Mandelbrot Set is mathematical sequence that is so complex and precise, full of infinite fractals, that it can only be recreated by computer.

Many people have also stated that they suddenly find a peculiar shape upon their bodies, such as a triangle. This is, again, a mathematical communication called 'Mathematical Proof', more specifically, the 'therefore' sign which is a syllogism (an instance of a form of reasoning in which a conclusion is drawn from two given or assumed propositions) meaning 'in conclusion'. It is indicating a logical consequence.

It is the short form of the Latin QED that translates to 'thus it is demonstrated' or 'to be shown'. Quite a specific and coded mathematical language for us to decipher.

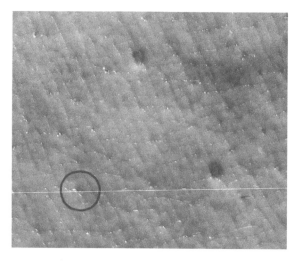

(Mathematical 'Therefore' Sign)

The reverse of this sign is the mathematical 'because' sign, which means 'logical reasoning' but connects to the therefore sign.

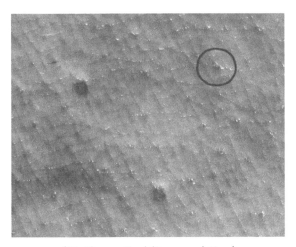

(Mathematical 'Because' Sign)

There are beings out there attempting to communicate, who are communicating, and who will continue to communicate by mathematics.

I, too, get mathematical communications. There have been many occasions recently when I have been given mathematical coded messages in my sleep state, even my awake state, in the form of either flashing or static number sequences. And, although I rarely remember my sleep state or dreams, these numbers have stuck with me as I awoke and throughout the day. One dreamtime vision was simply '√937', and I have worked hard to decode it.

Here goes:

The square root (√) of 937 = 30.6104557 (30.6) and 937 is the 13th 'star number'. A star number is a central figurate number representing a centred hexagram (6 pointed star). The 13th star number is as so, 12x12th triangular number +1...

The hexagram represents the ascent towards Godhead (Egyptian terminology for 'enlightened consciousness') and also represents insight, wisdom, and the magic power within.

In nature, the bee creates a honeycomb which is the shape of the hexagram. The bee is a symbol of Egyptian Royalty for this reason, and I have a deep connection to Ancient Egypt, having also been given its secret knowledge. Knowledge is material in the way that honey is material.

There was a secret work school that existed in Afghanistan for thousands of years called "Sarmoun Darq," which means "The Beehive" or the "Collectors of Honey." The purpose of this beehive was to collect human knowledge during the times when knowledge was dissipating and store it for future times when it could be used again. Most often undertaken in times of difficulty on earth, times of turmoil or war, this activity is so profound that most people cannot even conceive of what is involved and what significance it has. When we say the Sarmoun Darq stores human knowledge, we do not mean information. Information can be collected in books. There is no need to form a school or a secret society to store information. Unlike information, this knowledge is material in the way that honey is material. The knowledge is actually collected in the same way that bees collect nectar from flowers and change it into honey. This is why the school is called The Beehive; its function is to collect all kinds of nectars—aspects of essential knowledge.

The members have the capacity to concentrate it and change all the aromatic, beautiful nectars into very thick, sweet honey which they can then store in special flasks. When the right time comes, the flasks are opened and the knowledge is given out according to what is needed. The nectars are the different aspects of knowledge about Essence, and the honey is the distilled pure knowledge of Essence. The image of the bees and the honey and the hive and the nectar is the closest description of the actual reality of the school. It is the closest description of the actual reality because knowledge of Essence is material that can be collected, concentrated, and distilled. This becomes obvious when we understand that Essence actually exists just as honey exists, just as nectars exist. The real knowledge about Essence is Essence itself. Essence is itself the knowledge.

And all from a dream that wasn't a dream!

Another such example was again in a dream-state when I was given this symbol:

(mathematical 'Approximately Sign')

This is the mathematical 'Approximately Sign' which is also used to represent homeomorphism which is Topology, and Topology is how things relate to each other in space. It also deals with metric spaces and universe means 'one verse' and a verse is a metrical rhythm (metrical = relating to the metre). In other words the symbol was a coded message about the geometric spatial distances between universal objects and the creation of the universe in symbolic format. I saw the sign even down to the colour as displayed above, which is equal duality which gives us a universal parity. In universal terms positive and negative are treated equally.

The language of the universe is mathematics and, often, my dream-state and conscious state conversations are of a numerical nature.

Even the likes of the Bible is packed with numerical references that have been hidden within the scriptures for the interpretation of the initiates. That way, the general population cannot see what the chosen initiates can see and cannot know the sacred knowledge that the chosen initiates know. Religion is the perfect example of this double speak, where you have the stories taught to the congregations and then you have the truth, a truth hidden behind the fictional stories.

The likes of Plato taught sacred geometry and other sacred doctrine under the veil of secrecy to his chosen students at his academy. Secret doctrine was formulated and constructed in such a manner that it is incomprehensible to the vulgar, a masonic term for the ordinary person and he who is lacking sophistication. Sophistication derives from 'sophis' which is wisdom, therefore he who lacks wisdom. But the secret doctrine is easily interpreted by those possessing its key!

For this chapter, I will break down the individual sections of the main parts of the Anunnaki story, giving my interpretation of them as we go along so that it is easier to keep up with the comparisons.

I have not come across anyone else anywhere that has interpreted the story in the way that I have. To me, the whole story is a metaphor for geometric creation, which includes human genetics and, which, like everything else in the universe, has a geometric design. Pro-creation also plays a big part in this story, as does human consciousness.

I see a different version of the Sumerian scrolls than the version translated by Sitchen and I am now about to disclose my version of the story, which completely matches the message of all other ancient cultures of the time. It is a consistent theme that has been adopted throughout the ancient world. In Sanskrit the meaning of Anunnaki is anu (atom/atomic) and Nakin (god or one who possesses heaven) and Naka (heaven/sky). Therefore Anunnaki means life/atoms from heaven. It is telling us of our star origins.

The Anunnaki were reported to be giants, so let's start with the word 'giant'. Giant is a metaphor for a greater than average insight, a higher consciousness. Anu, who was the chief God of the Anunnaki, means 'Atom' in one of Earth's earliest languages, Sanskrit. Enki was the God of Water and wanted humans to have knowledge, water is symbolic of consciousness. In fact, the Anunnaki are also called the Watchers, which means 'Awake' or 'He who is Awake', and Sumer means 'land of the watchers'. They were also called the Nephilim, which derives from Naphal meaning 'falling short', and leads us onto biblical Sin, mentioned elsewhere in the book.

So what about the Sons of God and the Daughters of Men?

In Masonry, which is a Jewish establishment and also relevant biblically as the Bible is really the division of the Hebrew Scriptures, this phrase is really referring to the 'Spiral Dance', which is a DNA upgrade from a double helix to a triple helix genetic. It is ascension through a genetic DNA upgrade. It is referring to the procreation of the Male (Square) and the Earthly female (Masonic Compass logo).Consciousness gives us a godlike sense of the cosmos.

So, the statement that there were giants in those days, states in other words that there were those of a higher knowledge, a higher knowledge of self and the universe, who understood genetics (The Book of Genesis = The Book of Genetics/Book of Genes) and how to raise their own frequency in order to achieve the philosopher's stone, which is Enlightened Consciousness. This information is retained by the chosen initiates of past and present. Ancient cultures adopted the same reasoning and the same meaning in their systems of belief, all that changed was the names and locations, but the message remained the same across the whole ancient world.

Enlil was the God of Wind, and air/wind is the power of the mind, the force of intellect and knowledge, knowledge that he wanted to keep from humanity. We see many depictions of these Anunnaki Gods carrying a pinecone, which is really the pineal gland, our master gland, the third eye which is our inner illumination (enlightened consciousness). We also see them with wings and they are a replica of the 2 hemispheres, the 2 lateral wings of the cerebellum within the brain that deals with balance/ equilibrium which is essential in our quest for consciousness. In the brain, these lateral wings are separated by the Vermis which means serpent, which is why these Gods are depicted as serpents between two wings. A serpent man is symbolic of the God in Man or the God within us, and the pineal gland is known as the face of God.

This inner illumination, the solar force, is the lord of the body.

The strange watch that is often seen on the wrist of these Gods is the Merkabah, the wheel, the transport that takes you to a higher consciousness, the biblical chariot. And the strange looking handbag is multiple in meaning. The arch is the gateway beyond/ passage to another place. It is the bridge/inner or outer process, a link between man and God. The base of the handbag is the four, namely the material realm.

(Sumerian Tablets)

Genetically, the arch is 180 degrees, which is the perfect angle for hydrogen bonding and is what keeps the double helix of DNA together. Double helix has Enki and Enlil connotations, as you will see. 180 also gives us a coded message of 1+8+0=9. 9 is a pinnacle number. As I mentioned in the earlier stages of this book, I was shown a golden key in 2009 and began to understand its mysteries in 2019, both containing the number 9. The secrets of which are hidden inside the likes of religious books and secret societies through encryption, hidden from those who would seek to destroy the code. This System is guarded by an advanced encryption by numbers but also by intentions. Those who have the secrets are given the golden key. The 9 code was broken in music in the 1950's with a change in the harmonic frequency from 432 hertz (4+3+2=9) to 440 hertz (4+4+0=8). The mean average of all numbers in the universe is 9 and its cousin 11. The 9 code is also therefore written 911. 9 is how we escape the geometric matrix. I like Nikol Tesla had a fascination with the number 3, Tesla would walk around his hotel 3 times before entering and would only stay in a room where the number was devisable by 3. He noticed a

Nodal point (network) around the planet that involved 3,6 and 9.

In vortex maths (The Science Of Torus Anatomy) there is a repeating pattern of 1,2,4,8,7,5,1,2,4,8,7,5,1,2,4 and so on to infinity. 3,6,9 do not exist here as they are a vector from the third to the fourth dimension called the 'Flow-Field' which is a higher dimensional energy that influences the circuit of the other six numbers.

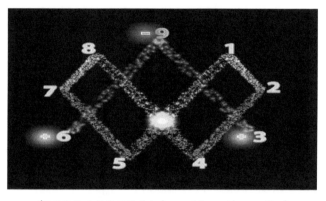

(0,1,2,3,4,5,6,7,8,9 is base 10 mathematics)

The gold circle is the number zero. 3 = energy, 6 = frequency and 9 = vibration. Vibrations of thirds, sixths and ninths are extraordinarily powerful. 3,6 and 9 is also encoded within the tetracyts which is how everything in the universe is structured. The harmonic number encoded within this is 432, 4+3+2=9. This same pattern continues inward and outward, both bigger and smaller toward infinity. It is the theorized underlying geometric structure of everything in the entire universe. If you put spheres around each tetrahedron of a 64 tetrahedron grid you get a 3D flower of life. The total number of degrees in the angles of a 64 tetrahedron grid is 25,920 which is the number of years in a procession of the equinox.

The number 9 is the finishing post and that which brings

completion, which is why we have 9 pyramids in Giza, 9 pyramids of 4 sides which gives us 9x4=36 and 3+6=9. It is a message by numbers. Even the human brain operates on bio-electrical transmissions. Therefore it can translate the impulses of electrical energy into sounds. When this was tested it was discovered that the brain kept repeating the phrase 'number 9'. 9 is used to hold a hidden code and 9 is the contruction of the universe. 9 is the god code. Even the speed of light at its messurement of metres per second, 299,792,458 contains 9 numbers. Humans are condensed light and so is our natural food. The numbers added together equals 55 which I will detail when I talk about time and the cesium atom later. 9 appears frequency in the ancient world, in the pyramids of Egypt and also biblical scripture, all of which are stated during the relevant chapters. We have been given the keys to the universe by a higher power.

Now back to the Anunnaki...

Another character of this story is Enlil's wife, Ninlil, who asked the Council of Seven to create Eridu (biblical Eden). 'Eden' means 'life', and the Garden of Eden is the human body. The Council of Seven are the 7 chakras that are the energy wheels of the human body itself. It is said that without the Council of Seven, Eridu would not exist, without our 7 chakras (Inner Council of Seven), the body (Eden/Eridu) would not exist.

The Sumerian story of Eridu introduces the characters of Adamu and Tiamat, which means 'sea of primordial creation'. This sea of creation also relates to sperm and semen (sea of men) and the planet Venus which, in Sanskrit, is called 'Shukra' meaning 'seminal secretion', all of which are associated with Enki. The story of Adamu and Taimat in Eridu is the biblical Adam and Eve. They lived in the East of Eden (East or Eridu), which is referring to the right side of the brain, the higher mind/consciousness. The Sumerian scrolls sometimes depict two serpents kissing, which is symbolic of the fusion of male and female power, our androgynous consciousness or, in the Sikh religion, the Kumara, which means 'androgynous serpent, the balance of opposites'.

In the Anunnaki story, it is stated that their home planet is Nibiru. In Egyptian astronomy, the planet Venus is called Neb-Heru. Many people have reported seeing two Suns in the sky and believe that it must be Nibiru, but there is a natural explanation for this, namely a phenomenon called 'Hunter's Moon' where the location of the Moon near the horizon causes the Hunter's Moon or any full Moon to look big and orange in colour. It gives us two Suns in appearance.

The scrolls do, however, really state that the Anunnaki's home planet is in fact Duku, which means 'Sacred Mound' and is referring to the Mons Veneris, meaning 'Mound of Venus' which is the pubic mound, again, a reference to fertility. The Anunnaki God, Enki, is also associated with semen and fertility.

'Nibiru' means 'crossing' or 'point of transition' in the Akkadian language and a transition means to change from one to another. In mammals, X and Y chromosomes determine sex. XX is female and XY is male. In females, one of the X chromosomes becomes inactive (XCI), resulting in X-link genes being equal in males and females. One X is silenced in every cell of a female embryo. XCI is X chromosome inactivation, known as lyonization. Males with an extra X are infertile. A cell must have consciousness to know that it has an extra X chromosome. There is also chromosomal translocation, which is an unusual arrangement. There are a number of different kinds of mutations when DNA is copied within a cell and passed onto the next generation called short-tandem repeats (STRs), also known as microsatellites. A mutation occurring in X-genes gives us an altered state, and genes passed between organisms in the same environment are called Horizontal Gene Transfer (HGT). Neb-Heru (Venus) is given the name Shukra in Sanskrit, which means seminal secretion. In other words sex, which then takes us back into chromosomes and Planet X. Nibiru is known as the 12th planet, according to Sitchen, and 12 means the end of something or the whole. The word 'planet' comes to us from a Greek element meaning passively drifting, wandering, or roaming.

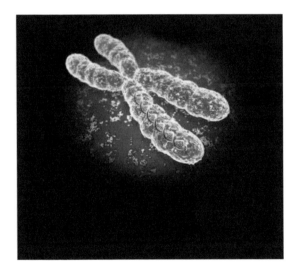

(Planet X)

X chromosomes move during mitosis, and mitosis is a cell division that results in two daughter cells each having the same number and same kind of chromosomes as the parent nucleus. X chromosomes contain our ancestral DNA. In Gemetria, which is the numerical value of words and letters, Planet X = 552 (X = 144) and the three letters of DNA = 114. 552+114=666=Man. 666

is the composition of carbon, 6 electrons, 6 protons, 6 neutrons, the carbon footprint which is man. When the 666 of carbon is combined with the elements (phosphate group) and mixed with Lucifer (Phosp-horus) we get a combination or reaction of chemical elements that forms DNA and RNA, this is the magical code for life. Phosphorus is Latin for Lucifer, and has the chemical element symbol of P. Phosphorus is an important chemical within DNA, consciousness and spiritual energy would not exist without it. The Chi-Rho are two bands that form the world soul (anima mundi) that crosses each other like the letter Chi. Phosphorus firing in the blood is the morning star. Phosphorus is red which is within our blood. Lucifer is therefore blood alchemy, the light bearer within our blood. The famous Alpha and Omega are phosphorus and the energy of fire that are worshipped by secret societies under the name of Lucifer and sometimes Baphomet. Phosphate is the only chemical that remains after death. Therefore we are born as alpha and die as the Omega.

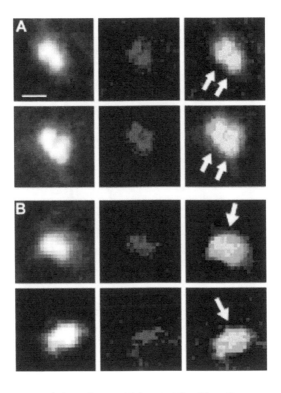

(Phosphorus Firing In The Blood)

666 is the sequence of DNA genetic signals or DNA fragments necessary for successful cloning. 6 is man which stops at 7, the perfect number. Phosphorus is the spark in DNA that makes fire. Ironically in internet terms all addresses start as www which we are told is the world-wide-web, but looking at it a different way. In Hebrew the letter W is Vav which has a numerical value of 6. Therefore www is 666.

(Arm position is the X = 1+4+4=9. It also indicates the union of opposites)

The 3600 orbit is really code for the reactivation of DNA = 36 is assisting humanity and 360 = PI. 3+6=9 = completion/esoteric man. X = 144 – 1+4+4=9, again giving the same message. The Sumerians said that a year on Planet Nibiru is equivalent in time to 3,600 years on Earth, which is the basis of atomic time.

The gold they sought was the philosopher's stone, the knowledge and wisdom of the third eye. This is the real Planet X, it is a genetic reference as in the whole Anunnaki story.

Now for even more genetic reference with this misinterpreted picture overleaf:

(Sumerian Tablet, depicting the planets... or something else?)

Many people state and believe that this picture represents the planets but I am going to now show you otherwise. It is really genetic and not planetary. At the centre you can see the 6 pointed star also known as the hexagram. And at the heart of every hexagram there is its nuclear hexgram, which this center star represents. The 11 other stars is also important as it is telling us of the hexagram 11 meaning Qian, heaven and Kun, earth, in other words heaven and earth, and in some circles the word annunaki means those who from heaven to earth came, it is talking about humanity which came from the stars. Nuclear means the nucleus of an atom or the energy released in nuclear fusion or fission. The hexagram represents the ascent towards godhead, insight and wisdom and the magic power within. The hexagram 11 is the inner and outer trigrams forming earth over heaven. It resembles the universe as DNA is the universe.

The Sitchen version of the story states that the Anunnaki brought the Moon to Earth's current orbit but, scientifically, this could not have been the case and there is scientific example after example that proves this not to be the case.

One of these is that the Moon and Earth have the same oxygen isotopes, which mean that they originated at the same distance from the Sun, and the fact that there are what is known as 'tidal rhythmites' on Earth that prove an astronomical induced tidal influence over 2.2 billion years ago, the Moon powers the tides of Earth therefore it was there at least 2.2 billion years ago. The Anunnaki were said to have brought the Moon to its current position 450,000 years ago which, again, is inconsistent with Earth science. There are many other examples too, such as mathematics. The solar system is what it is and the Moon was not brought here as an after-thought.

Basically, without the Moon, there is no life on Earth, no seasons, no liquid water, and no habitable temperature for life and, seeing as the story states that the Anunnaki found life upon Earth as they arrived, this cannot be correct. More about this in a moment.

Enki and Enlil were known as the Sheti, which means 'Snake Brothers', the double helix of human DNA that intertwine like two serpents, one positive and one negative. DNA double helix has a positive and negative polarity of opposite twist. Enki is the positive serpent and Enlil is the negative serpent. And yet, we are told by history that scientists Watson and Crick discovered the DNA double helix in 1953. The Sumerian scrolls told us about it many thousands of years ago.

The face on Mars, which the story states is a character called Alulu, the supervisor of the gold mining expedition, is referring to wave genetics and our DNA originally starts off as a genetic wave. 'Alulu' means 'waveform', which DNA changes from in order to become DNA. It is wave genetics, and wave genetics has shown that genetic traits can be changed, activated, and deactivated by use of resonant waves beamed at the DNA. Wave genetics is the process of using resonant waves and certain electromagnetic waves to affect the genes in DNA. DNA begins as a pulsating wave of invisible genetic information, whose waves create microscopic gravitational forces that pull in atoms and molecules from their surrounding environment to construct DNA, which is called 'wave genetics'.

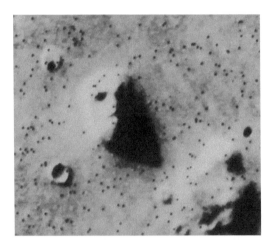

(Face on Mars – Alulu)

THE ANUNNAKI DID NOT BRING THE MOON

One aspect of the Anunnaki story is that when they arrived on Earth, they brought with them the satellite known as the Moon. It also states in the same text that when they arrived here, they found life on Planet Earth!

This cannot be correct for many reasons, which I will now at times repeat and at other times outline a few new examples.

The Moon keeps the Earth at a 23.5 degree tilt, which keeps her waters/oceans as a liquid and not a solid. This tilt acts as a planetary stabiliser and gives us the four seasons along with planet-inhabiting warmth.

Both the Earth and the Moon have the same isotopes, which are chemical elements, and they are the same age. Therefore, they were created at the same time in the same region of space that they now occupy. The Moon is exactly 400 times smaller than the Sun and exactly 400 times closer to Earth, therefore giving us the phenomenon of an eclipse. If we divide the circumference of the Sun by that of the Moon and multiply by 100, we get the polar circumference of Earth. The Moon revolves at exactly 100th of the speed that the Earth turns on its axis.

Therefore, it is mathematical creation to be that way and the Sun, Earth, Moon trinity is amazing. The Moon was not a subsequent addition; it was a deliberate origin of the 'One Time Beginning', there from the start of the region of space known as the solar system. The whole universe is an intentional mathematical canvas. There is also a planetary trinity between the Sun, the Moon, and Earth, which makes it totally by design that these planets have always been where they are now.

Now For More 400 – 100 Mathematics: The ancients thought that it was magic, modern astronomers don't tell you about it, and social education hides many secrets.

When we look up at the night sky and see stars, planets, galaxies, nebulas, and other spatial phenomenon, what do we see? Are we blindly gazing into the darkness of space, which is really full and not empty, or are we letting ourselves look beyond the canopy and the canvas with a thinking, wandering mind?

I have stated a number of times that the universe follows mathematical codes and is numerical by design, which encompasses sound, light, and geometry, which are all members of the same family.

But there is a phenomenon much closer to home that we are never informed of, and that phenomenon is the 400-100 mathematics of the Sun, Earth, and Moon trinity... That trinity follows a deliberate mathematical design that cannot be by chance.

I first began looking into the Moon and its connections to Earth when I was researching the work of Zecharia Sitchen and his translation of the Sumerian Anunnaki scrolls, which stated that this extra-terrestrial race brought the Moon to Earth from across the cosmos and, when arriving at Earth, they found life already here. I soon worked out that this could not have been the case based on planetary science. The Moon is also rotating at a rate of 400km per Earth day. The Moon revolves at exactly 100th of the speed that the Earth turns on its axis. When we divide the circumference of the Sun by that of the Moon and multiple by 100, we get the polar circumference of Earth. When we divide the size of the Sun with that of Earth and multiple by 100, we get the size of the Moon.

This is staggering and a deliberate mathematical design. The whole universal make-up is by the design of a mathematical genius with a genius purpose.

It makes no sense to me that this race would travel to Earth, which means that they had an independent trajectory, to be in Earth's orbit (seemingly locked in) to come back around again every 3600 years. If they have a trajectory - and they must have to get here - then why can't they leave? Why would they go to the extreme hardship of creating a new human race to mine for them, when they could simply blast the likes of asteroid Eros which has more gold than has ever been found on Earth? If something doesn't make sense, there is usually a reason for it; it didn't happen that way!

Eros has 20,000 billion kilograms of gold. There would have been a much simpler way than the route they allegedly took.

AND THOSE WHO FROM HEAVEN TO EARTH CAME: THAT IS REALLY HUMANITY

In Hebrew, Heaven is the Shamayim (superior waters), and when certain letters are removed from this Hebrew word, it becomes the Mayim, which are the waters of Earth and body.

It is according to their scriptures where God resides as 'Yud', the gift, or holy seed, which then takes us straight back to fertility, as the holy seed is sperm, the life in the waters. Sperm, which means seed, is anointed by semen (sea of men) in the creational waters, which then takes us to the Biblical Jesus, the anointed one. Jesus, in the Anunnaki story, was an incarnation of Enki. This is really esoterically talking of a fertility, Venus, Sperm, and a semen connection.

Enki's sacred number is 40 which, again, has a 'Jesus in the wilderness for 40 days and nights' connotation. 40 is also the number that lifts you to a spiritual state, and remember that Enki wanted to impart knowledge upon humanity.

And now for more on the face on Mars and the Alulu story.

It is quite apparent that there either has been, or still is, life on Mars. We can see it with the Cydonian city, which has geometric structures such as the five-sided pyramid. The number five is, of course, the pentagram, which is 'realised man'.

I firmly believe that there is a greater force at work here, a force that is telling us of our origins and our potential, and I firmly believe that there is a message far greater than one extra-terrestrial race. I could well and truly subscribe to the idea that it is the mathematical creator itself.

The human body is designed by the geometric 'golden ratio', sometimes called the 'golden mean', amongst others. The human face is exclusively the golden ratio (golden section). Even the womb, the seat of life, is also the golden ratio.

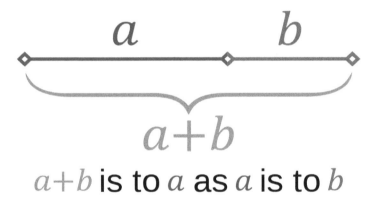

$$a + b \text{ is to } a \text{ as } a \text{ is to } b$$

(Golden Ratio = Union/Marriage Of Body And Spirit)

I think the face contains a hidden clue to our geometric design. This face, or so we are told in the Sitchen translation, was Alalu the supervisor of the mining expedition. So, where does Alulu fit into the subject? The name 'Alulu' in Telugu means 'wave genetics', a genetic wave, a vibration, waveform and wave genetics is a process of using resonant waves and certain electromagnetic waves to affect the genes in DNA. DNA begins as a waveform, pulsating waves of invisible genetic information whose waves create microscopic (also the meaning of Alulu) gravitational forces that pull in atoms (ANU) and molecules from their surrounding environment to construct DNA (wave genetics).

DNA's double helix (Enki & Enlil – snake brothers) is forever covered by water molecules that attach themselves by hydrogen bonds (Enki – God of Water).

The height of one unit of DNA helix (Enki and Enlil) is related to its width in a proportion equal to the golden spiral/ratio. The golden ratio divides a line into a 62%/38% separation and the Greek Gemetria (numerical value of letters/words) of Jesus Christ is 2368, which are the digits of the percentage numbers. Jesus, according to the Anunnaki story, was an incarnation of Enki, and Christ consciousness (higher level of human consciousness) is hidden within the golden ratio.

The golden section is also based within the Fibonacci sequence, which is the balance of the natural world and the third dimension.

Another group in the Anunnaki story are the Igigi. They were described as a group of heavenly spirits under the God, Anu. A spirit is the non-decaying spin of the electron (atom/anu). The Igigi seem to have been a lower rank of Gods. They were a servant class which existed before human beings were created, until they rebelled after 40 days (40 = lift to a spiritual state). The aspect of this that stands out to me is the fact that the Sitchen translation tells us that there were 300 Igigi in Heaven. Again, this is both a consciousness story and a genetics story that happens in each and every one of us. When you look at the Bible, which is a division of the Hebrew Scriptures (script), it talks about sin and being born with original sin. The word 'sin' derives from the Hebrew word 'shin' (Mr Spock's hand gesture in *Star Trek* is its symbol). Shin has a numerical value of 300. Shin is the three primary forces and the fiery aspect of those forces which are the universal forces of positive, negative, and neutral. It is known as the 'Triune Atomic Fire', and that is our three sub-atomic particles within our atom (anu). The number 3 is hidden within shin within us. This is also the Enki and Anu connection of sky and Heaven as human atoms are the same as universal atoms. In bodily terms, Heaven is the upper chakras, especially the mind, the crown chakra, and the third eye region. This is the 300 in heaven, it is the Hebrew shin. We are all born with original shin (sin) as we are all born with the universal holy trinity within us. This is also the biblical story of the 300, the Persian army.

CONCLUSION:

Aliens exist, or at least what we deem as aliens. Some of them have a solid texture and those who vibrate at a higher frequency have a lighter body. In reality, 99.9999999% of everything is really a vacuum, and not solid at all. What we think of as solid matter is just condensed light, and light is an electromagnetic frequency. All forms and shapes and sizes exist, I have seen at least one species here walking amongst us on Earth and other people have seen other species. I have seen too many things in our skies to know that there is a presence we are not being told about by our authorities.

The whole ancient world has documented encounters with these beings from another world, culture after culture have recorded it and, in a universe so large and seemingly endless, how could Earth humans possibly be the only existence? It is such a narrow way of thinking, and it deserves little time here. When you look into the mathematical work of Carl Munck, you see that the famous monuments on Earth such as Stonehenge in the UK and the pyramids in Giza, Egypt, have encoded, within their grid vectors, the location of both the famous face on Mars and also the Cydonian city, again, on Planet Mars. In an additional twist, these Martian monuments also contain, encrypted within their grid vectors, the location of Stonehenge and the Giza pyramids. On the Moon, we also have what is called the 'Lunar Abaka', which is a set of six obelisks that have connections to the three main pyramids of Giza in Egypt. The obelisk is the symbol of Egyptian God, Osiris, it is the phallus.

This can only mean one of two things, either the same civilisation had a method of galactic travel and travelled between these planets, or a greater civilisation visited Earth from the stars and gave advanced knowledge to certain people of Earth. In fact, in some rarely seen Egyptian hieroglyphs, you can see carvings of extra-terrestrial beings amongst the Egyptian hierarchy.

This sacred knowledge is written in the guise of, and in the form of, metaphors, allegories, codes, and symbols. I can see these codes and metaphors throughout the world, both the ancient world and now the modern day.

The Sumerian scrolls are no different to that list. They are metaphorical of a higher type of genetics that is humanity. I believe that there is a greater force and influence at play here, maybe even the creator that is leaving clues for us to follow.

One thing is clear to me; the universe is not empty space, it is space that is teeming with life of various forms.

We are part of that space and we are a part of everything that it comprises of. We have allowed ourselves to disengage, and we have drifted so far from the shore that we no longer associate the beach with the ocean.

I think that Sitchen has done what many of those in the know have done before him, and that is to mislead humanity in order to cover up a much greater truth, the brilliance that is ourselves.

You are everything.

MODERN SCIENCE IS AN ANCIENT KNOWLEDGE

Ancient monuments were placed at certain locations, usually upon Earth's leylines, which are areas of heightened magnetic fields. Magnetic fields are information carriers, just like sound waves. Leylines are energetic arterial routes, and leylines are landlines which is a name we give to modern day devices, namely phones connected within our homes. In Celtic Geomancy, leylines are called the dragon, and one such example is the St. Michael's leyline that spans the south of England, this is the famous George and the Dragon story. George is on top of the dragon and is therefore its master, which I will detail more later in the Stonehenge chapter. 'George' means 'worker of the land', and it is the mastery of your inner fire. 'England' means 'land of angles', and leylines are geometric alignments, which are angles. The stones continually absorb the earth energy through their base which is rooted in the ground. Using their internal crystal lattice, the stones can process and convert earth energy into an aerial form of electromagnetic ley-energy, which can be likened to a beam of linear energy. This is why beams of light have been seen emanating from the top of certain pyramids.

As you will see later in the Stonehenge chapter, reverberating ringstones which are activated by a tonal rill, voice harmonics, are ringtones, it is just a restructure of the letters of the word. It was, in effect, a download through overtone singing, harmonising self, and making the stones sing back.

The ancient world communicated with each other through Earth's magnetic lines that acted as a network of communication. They used crystalline within the monoliths, as we use silicon in modern day computers. They were also a communication system to and from the stars. This is one of the ways in which they all had the same knowledge base, and were encrypting this knowledge base into their designs.

We are being left the tools to transcend this third dimension but, firstly, we must reactivate ancient wisdoms. One such clue is the Giza Plateau, which contains 9 pyramids of 4 sides. This gives us 9x4=36. In Numerology, the number 36 relates to assisting humanity. This will become more apparent in the Egypt chapter later. These monuments were put there by the elder race of man from Orion, and the clue to this is written in the alignment with Orion's belt. These sacred places were used by those chosen to known how to use them. However, this sacred knowledge was retained by the few and kept hidden from the masses, and the true interpretation was left for only those who knew how to interpret the ancient wisdoms.

FOUR

THE SECRETS OF EGYPT

Egypt is a pinnacle land and a pinnacle civilisation, and they held advanced knowledge used by many other societies that also made their knowledge base advanced. Greece and its philosophers were Egyptian Mystery School initiates, and even the Kabballah was influenced by Egypt.

Egypt was the prerequisite for Christianity, Horus was the original Jesus, and Isis was the original Mary.

The symbol of Christianity is the fish, but this has connections to the pre-Christ Egyptian God, Horus. Horus gives us the word 'Horizon' (Horus-Risen), which has relevance to Astronomy and the solar Sun, the cosmic Christ. Although I don't delve too much into astronomy in this book, it has its place, and its influence is shown none more so than Christmas Day, 25th December, which is the day that the Sun moves for the first time in three days (dead for 3 days) north to continue its annual transit. On December 22nd, 23rd and 24th, the Sun remains in the same degree of sky. The movement of the Sun on 25th December is why we have Christmas Day on that particular date around most of the world. The 25th December also gives us a mathematical code of 2+5+1+2=10. 10 is the completion of God's divine order which is also built into our anatomy as base 10 mathematics; 10 fingers and 10 toes. The Christmas tree symbolises the spinal column. All the lights on the Christmas tree represent the senses of the soul that we need to awaken in order to perceive what Christ is, and the star at the top is the pentagram.

I am now going to show you a coded connection between the fish of Christianity and Horus, namely The Eye of Horus.

The Christian fish derives from the centre of the vesica piscis, which I will detail later when I reveal the identity of Mary Magdalene.

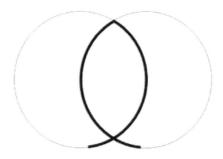

(When turned 90 degrees, which is a quarter (¼), it becomes this.)

(That 90 degree turn (1/4) is important.)

(The Eye of Horus.)

The shape of the Christian fish also makes The Eye of Horus and, more interestingly, by placing a pupil inside the fish you get The Eye of Horus mathematically because, in Egyptian fractions, the pupil is ¼.

The Eye of Horus is the pineal gland, spiritual sight, within the brain. It is the horizontal oval containing the mandala (eye). The eye takes the outside world to the inner and can also project the inner world onto the outer. This is also within the Supreme Court in the UK, only visible from an aerial view of the interior of the courtroom.

Much of what you are about to learn has been missed by mainstream Egyptologists and scholars alike. I have talked about alchemy, which originates in Egypt formally known as Khem, from where we get the word alchemy, the chemistry of God. I have discussed the Kabballah, which is a branch of the Ancient Egyptian principles, altered to suit, and I am about to discuss in the next chapters Christianity, which also contains many of the Egyptian principles. Ancient Egypt is a basis for many Christian ideologies, such as the Sun, which is the cosmic Christ. So, to me, it represents a good place to start.

With that said, I felt it right to touch upon this mystical place, the place that sees millions of tourists each year, all pondering what and why. The place that sees numerous documentaries and movies about it, and the place where no-one seems to have knowledge of the why. This chapter may be revealing to you if you are one of those people!

Before I went to Egypt on vacation in 2010, a vacation that Sarah and I both knew wasn't just a holiday, I was contacted by a psychic medium from Scotland in the UK. She told me that she had a message from her spiritual council, a message I am about to share with you. I will not mention her name as I have no permission to do so, but I didn't know her and had never met her. She made contact out of the blue, much to my surprise.

This is that message, word for word:

"Regarding your trip to Egypt

You will help uncover more insights and translate ancient knowledge brought to us from great distance. Under the Sphinx lies an ancient secret knowledge that will be added to your toolbox.

Use this wisely for the benefit of all, all meaning past, present and future. It all belongs together, in the same place.

You must absorb, accept, understand and finally know. Only then can you share and teach."

(Psychic Medium in 2010)

This was a special message and, although I went inside the Great Pyramid, stood next to the Sphinx, went to the Cairo Museum, ventured down the Nile, and spent time in the desert with the Bedouin tribe, I saw no evidence of what the message meant. Amazingly though, we had been told that we needed to be as close to the right-hand side of the Sphinx as possible. The area was crowded, making us just like sardines in a shiny can but, as Sarah and I approached the Sphinx, to the right-hand side, a gap just big enough for two people opened up at that exact point, which Sarah and I just slipped into, as if it had been ordained and made to happen. There was barely any standing room anywhere, apart from the gap that had just appeared for us. Coincidence or not, it made for an interesting talking point.

The message was perplexing, and I had naturally expected some kind of incident to match the words that never actually, or seemingly, materialised. However, seven years later, all became perfectly clear and that message now held meaning.

And it was worth the wait. I was now getting ancient knowledge placed into my head and mind day after day, and it was forming that ancient Gnostic blueprint that I previously spoke about. I was being given information that no-one else seemed to be talking about, none of the great researchers and speakers were mentioning the secrets I was being given, and I am not even going to mention the Ancient Egyptian visitations I was receiving around that time. Something had happened in 2010, a key had been used to open a doorway within me, a doorway that I didn't even know existed for seven years.

Seven years is, ironically, a number of the end of something before we enter into eight, which is also the number one as a beginning. It certainly was a new beginning for me.

A LITTLE BIT ABOUT THE TRIP:

So, the time had arrived and we landed on Egyptian soil in the blistering winter heat, trips booked and at the ready. The day had also now arrived for us to take a 4am flight to Cairo, early on in the vacation, and that day was to be a memory forged forever as we visited the museum there, seeing mummies over 3000 years old that looked better than I did since I'd had an early start that day!

Ancient artefacts, like King Tutankhamun's death mask, shone out at us in their golden splendour. We enjoyed lunch on the Nile, in a boat of course, before the main spectacle, the pyramids. As we drove around Cairo in our coach packed with tourists, I lost count of the near misses with the bumper-to-bumper traffic, horses, and other wandering animals. But then, I saw what I had come to see. Through the gaps in the building line the most familiar shape associated with this land: the tetrahedron pyramid in all its glory, adjacent to McDonald's as modern day capitalism stood shoulder to shoulder with ancient giants.

I jumped off the coach. Having heard mainstream renditions of the reasons for the pyramids - burial tombs for Pharaohs, the most recited - I knew this was completely incorrect, but nevertheless an interesting topic of debate.

I eventually passed beggars and corrupt officials as I made my way to the Great Pyramid and ventured inside for a brush with claustrophobia as I twisted and turned inside the narrow spaces.

Then, after soaking in many thousands of years of history in minutes of modern time, I made my way towards the guardian, the Sphinx, the route taken by many ancient initiates of the Mystery Schools of advanced knowledge and wisdom, a route walked with a sense of inner familiarity across the desert sands. Desert derives from the Egyptian word 'Deshret' (DSHRT), meaning 'red lands'.

As you approach the pyramids in the Giza Plateau, you have to negotiate the famous Sphinx, a journey undertaken by many initiates of the ancient mysteries all those thousands of years ago. So much invisible sacred geometry intrinsic within its design, all with an esoteric meaning, one of consciousness. But what does it all mean?

You will not get the answer to that question from mainstream schooling, Egyptologists, or scholars. But you will get it from books like this. The whole ethos of the Ancient Egyptian culture and all others that I have researched, which spread across the world in such places as Greece, where many of the great philosophers were initiates of the Egyptian Mystery Schools, such as Pythagoras. And, of course, the likes of the Kabbalah and mystical Judaism which forms the hidden secrets of the Bible is a higher type of human. Enlightened consciousness was also key in this journey of the self.

For those with the knowledge of mind and matter, such as the

Pharaohs and the Priesthoods, life would have been a different experience. They believed themselves to be physical incarnations of the Sun-Gods, they were the walking knowledge, also believing that such sacred knowledge was an honour and a privilege and not a general right. It had to be earned, which has been the underlying principle of the higher society levels of the ancients throughout history. And this is still true of today amongst the priesthoods, the brotherhoods, and the higher ranks of the societies with secrets (secret societies). They knew about, and had a deep understanding of, body and mind, the universe, genetics, harmonics, and consciousness, and how to attain the God-state of being, travelling out of body to what they deemed the 'other world'.

In order to know these things, the Egyptians must have had access to the sophisticated scientific equipment used today in the 21st century, or even had access to a greater knowledge base that they could tap into to retrieve such insight. They knew that in order to reach divinity, the balance of opposites, namely duality, had to take place. They needed to bring equilibrium to the material and physical realm with harmony in order to be able to transcend out of it. They saw the physical and metaphysical as the two lands balanced by the 'sema-tawy' (from where we get the word 'cemetery'), as the two worlds meet through ourselves from our transition from physical life to physical death. They knew about chemistry and alchemy which both derive from Al-khem, meaning the way of Egypt. The two opposites of duality were to be balanced by the chemical marriage of King and Queen, referred to as 'Tying the Knot', a phrase used today in modern day wedding ceremonies but without any idea of its origin.

(Tying The Knot.)

The Sphinx is the sacred symbolism of the four creatures of alchemy, also known as the four biblical creatures of Eden and even the four beasts. The Sphinx is a symbol of the elements. The paws of the lion are related to fire, the wings of the eagle to the air, the face of the human being to the water, and the legs of the bull to the earth (lion is also sight). It is the four Gospels and the realisation of Magnum Opus, the Great Work of alchemy. The broken nose/nose destroyed, which is deliberate, signifies ignorance of the mysteries of sexual alchemy or 'Pranayama', which is breath control. The water erosion below the sphinx is also deliberate and is symbolic of the dissolution of the material form and the release from the confines of matter. What is left is the enlightened King. Wings are also symbolic of a higher than human condition transcending.

In the four Gospels, Matthew = Man/Water - Mark = Lion/Fire – Luke = Bull/Earth – John = Eagle/Air. It is forces of the four gathered into one. Of course, when you look into Hebrew, you see that their God, Yahweh (Yod-He-Vau-He), is the four elements, and Yahweh

(YHWH) is the divine force within the four elements. In Latin, this is given the name of Jehovah (JHVH). Fighting the bull, as they do in Spain, is really symbolic of overcoming your animal instinct; the bull is not meant to be slayed, it is meant to be tamed and controlled.

The gigantic Sphinx is indicating to us that we need to overcome our animalistic nature/soul in order to become human. The Sphinx is 240 foot long and 66 foot high, and this gives us 2+4+0=6 and 66, all making 666, the number of the beast/man. This forms part of the initiations and the balance of self in order to progress. No-one who acts and behaves like its animalistic soul will be the vessel to become human. Animals act with instinct, without thinking, whereas humans have the ability to think before they act. An animal will kill another animal out of necessity for food, or sometimes because it can. Acting without thinking, whether that is right or wrong, as they do not have that ability (Abel). A human can make those choices based on conscious and conscientious thought. This takes us back to Cain and Abel; do you think before acting, or do you act first without thinking?

The Sphinx is the gateway to the pyramidal initiations for those who have acquired human status.

The Sphinx is the esoteric path, the sacred way that we must tread - namely the mysteries of the ninth sphere, sex - through work with the four elements of nature within ourselves to become the human being (I will talk more about the ninth sphere later). The Sphinx's eagle wings are the air that penetrates through the nose of the Sphinx. The symbolic door, or the entry into the mysteries of the Sphinx, is on the nose, which is the breath of life. Nostrils are connected to the testicles and the ovaries, hence why breathing techniques are used in the likes of tantric practices. The nose, lips, and mouth are gnosis/knowledge. Transforming and channelling sexual energy is breath technique. Control of the nostrils is control of sexual matter. 'Spirit' in Latin derives from the word 'spiritus', which means 'breath'. Therefore, spirituality is the art of breathing. The soul in Greek is the word 'psykhe', which is where we also get the word 'psyche'. The soul is within the human mind and is housed in the pineal gland. It is the power of kings that enters the psyche, and the word 'Royal' means 'God-King'. The sphinx is the forces of the four elements gathered in one force or the elemental divine force within the four elements. And it tells us of the great work that must be performed with the four elements.

Egyptian statues, like many ancient statues around the world, usually have their left foot forward and this is indicating, esoterically, that they have hermetic, or specialist, knowledge. When we see the likes of the famous four statues sitting with their palms upon their thighs, this is indicating the dominion over regeneration. The four, of course, is the material realm, the four elements that must be overcome to reach the fifth element, the God source. This is why Pharaohs sit upon a square cubic throne to indicate that they have mastery over the four.

(Statues of Abu Simbel)

Egyptian body postures are geometry of the body that take you into harmonic resonance with different universal energies that induce enlightenment.

Many Egyptian Gods have the heads of birds, which is symbolic of a higher level of mind that has been purified. The head of a falcon is the highest of the levels of objective reasoning (Logic) that any initiate can develop, called Anklad. When someone reaches Anklad, they receive the head of a falcon. Horus is the falcon-headed God. It is this objective reasoning and logic, which is associated with the north in cardinal points, that the Great Pyramid faces due north.

The base of the pyramid is the four elements and its apex the fifth element which contained a golden capstone illustrating completion of Magnum Opus, the Great Work of alchemy, better known as the philosopher's stone. So why are there nine pyramids? In alchemy, there are nine divisions from the three essences of Mercury, Sulphur, and Salt. Each of these essences contain the other two, which forms the law of the triangle where two components come together to produce the third. This is why Mercury has been found in the pyramid of Teotihuacán, they were practising transmutation through alchemy which is alchemical ascension. After this process, salt is all that remains of the body, which is symbolic of the biblical Lot's wife turning to salt.

Therefore, with this in mind, we get 3+3+3 = 9, 9 being completion and the number of esoteric man. When we add Azoth, the eternal fire, the Krestos (Christ), we get the number 10, which is why we have the 10 Commandments and even number 10 Downing Street, the British Prime Minister's residence in London. The famous door is covered in this esoteric symbology with its black door representing Saturn and the start of magnum opus leading to the Sun's rays near to the top of the door which is the gold of wisdom and the philosopher's stone and, of course, we have the number 10, which is the 9 divisions of alchemy plus Azoth = 10. The figure 10 is in white, and white gives us the marriage of Heaven and Earth (Union of Opposites) and the complete removal of separation. There are 9 pyramids, each containing 4 sides, which gives us 9x4=36. 36 in numerology is assistance to humanity, 36 also gives us 3+6=9, the number 9 that esoteric number of completion again. The pyramids are our key out of the third dimensional world.

The 9+1 gives us the Pythagorean decad.

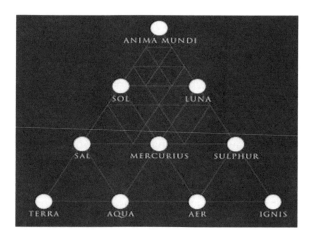

(Pythagorean Decad)

The anima mundi is the world soul which, when reached, causes everything in creation to become one and then "the *Lion shall lie down with the lamb*".

In Egypt, the chief deity is Atum, which comes from 'Tem', meaning 'completion'. He is the head of the Ennead, meaning 'nine'. And now, onto mummies. Many mummies demonstrate the symbol of Osiris, which is the crossed arms across the heart region. The crossed arms are the pivot point and the union of opposites. It also shows the four cardinal directions/four elements. In Egypt, opposites are in pairs. This then leads us onto the axis mundi. The axis mundi, meaning 'axis of the mound', is the trunk of the tree of life. A mummy is symbolic of the encasement within the trunk, which is the world tree and the point of connection between earth and sky (Heaven).

Part 5 of the 7 stages of alchemy has two processes, which are fermentation and putrefaction. Putrefaction is the decomposition of our former selves, the process of inner death by which the old elements of conscious and unconscious minds are allowed to rot and decompose. Fermentation then occurs, which is the rebirth of self.

That is why a vineyard (wine) is a symbol of higher consciousness because, at a certain stage of fermentation, we transform just like wine. I will deal with water into wine later in the book. The bodily organs were placed into the four canopic jars, which are the five inner Gods of Taoism, known as the five Viscera. Organs of the main bodily cavities are where Gods were believed to reside.

The axis mundi is also the tree of Eden situated in the centre of the garden. It is the middle tree, the world axis, or world pillar. The axis mundi is symbolised by the oak tree, the most sacred of trees. The Celtic name for oak is 'daur' from where we get 'door', hence the oak tree being the doorway to another world and a journey to enlightenment. The word 'Druid' derives from 'Dru-Wid', which means 'knower of oak trees of oak knowledge'. The word 'tree' derives from 'Treow', which means 'true', therefore 'tree knowledge' means 'true knowledge'. Trees are upright, and were associated with truth. The Islamic God, Allah, comes from 'Elah' which means 'oak' (or 'an oak'), translated in Hebrew as 'Terebinth', which means 'tree'. Therefore, Allah is a phrase that describes the journey to enlightenment, again, metaphorical.

This makes even more sense when you know that the abode of Allah is where the three sacred rivers meet. Those rivers are the Ida, Pingala, and Shushumna - the energy channels of the body - and they meet at the third eye, the seat of spiritual sight. On every mosque, you will find the crescent moon, which is the alchemical symbol of silver. Silver is associated with the sixth chakra, the third eye. Allah has also been associated with the Moon God, Sin. This is the esoteric reason behind it. In the Egyptian language, 'Allah' means 'the moon'. There are the public levels of knowledge and then there is the real knowledge and the real truth and there is a big difference.

It is intrinsic within all of the world religions, but to say so brings accusations of blasphemy, how people have such limited vision, which is of course how they, the heads of these belief systems, get away with creating multi-tiered faith systems.

Each year we have Ramadan which is the period of Islamic fasting! But did you know that there are two types of fasting? Exoteric fasting which is abstention from food/drink, keeping your mouth closed so as not to eat or drink. And there is esoteric fasting that the likes of the Sufi's do. Sufism is mystical Islam. Esoteric fasting is keeping your mouth closed to abstain from speaking of the esoteric knowledge of revelation and interpretation to those who lack the capacity to receive it. Fast = Ruza = keep secret.

The practice of concealing sacred knowledge is called Taqiyyah.

Something may be hidden because of its immense value, or to

be reverently concealed from the prying eyes of the profane, the profane are the vulgar, the unsophisticated who lack knowledge.

Spiritual knowledge is like food and light:

Just as a small child needs to be fed gradually, stage by stage, until it reaches adolescence, so that it may not eat something detrimental to its constitution, and just as light is appropriate only to persons with open, healthy and strong eyes, so that a person whose eyes have been shut, or had just emerged from darkness, will be severely dazzled by daylight, in the same way, those who get hold of this knowledge should communicate it only to those who are in need of it. Those are deemed to be the chosen initiates who are the ones who can interpret the mysteries correctly.

Your religious characters are not real people and never were, the heads of religion know this but have concealed their sacred and secret knowledge by using the facade of iconic characters taught as being real.

Still on the theme of the axis mundi: The Quatrefoil seen at many Churches represents the cosmic central axis between the four cardinal points, the axis mundi, the world center and axis mundi means the world axis. It is the connection between heaven and earth. It is the passageway between the celestial world and the underworld.

The axis mundi, also known as the world tree, is symbolised by the most sacred of trees, the Oak tree.

(Quatrefoil)

Now I shall move onto the meaning of the pyramids and what they really represent, before covering some more Egyptian secrets, such as the elongated skulls.

When you break down the word 'pyramid', in Gnostic circles, you get 'Pyra' meaning 'fire', 'Am' or 'Om' represents God and, in the Hindu religion, 'om' is the primordial sound that created the universe, 'om' being their word for the Sun which has a root word of 'sound/sonic'. The mantra of 'am', 'aum', or 'om' is the name of God, or the vibration of the Supreme when the vibration of the mantra is spoken correctly and in the correct vibrational tone. Id is the mind and the psyche residing within unconsciousness, namely instinct and impulse and, as previously stated, these are animalistic traits. Therefore, we get 'pyramid' as the *'fire of God in the mind'*. We are now entering the meaning of the pyramids, the fire within, Christ/Krestos, which is enlightenment. The triangle/ pyramid shape is also the symbol of the element of fire. The word 'Pharaoh' means 'great house', and a house is synonymous with the mind.

'RA' gives us 'Ram', which is code for mind-light (enlightenment) and is the reason why we have such Egyptian Pharaonic names as Ramesses. This is the meaning of the biblical *Lamb of God'.* 'RA' in Hebrew is 'Resh and Ayin'. 'Resh' means 'head', and 'Ayin' means 'eyes of vision'. When we fall into the temptation of the descending serpent (Satan - I will detail this later in the book), we awaken Ayin, the vision within the head related to the pineal and pituitary gland. Awakening Resh and Ayin gives insight but, if consciousness is awakened within ego, God is not there. This is our demon, our developed powers with ego still alive.

Consciousness within ego is Baalism, meaning 'lord' and is a term for 'Sirs', a title given to those knighted by the Queen of England and other royals. Incidentally, the concept of royalty stems from Ancient Egypt, hence the numerous Egyptian symbology around royal insignia and alike.

Ayin, the vision within the head, is related to the pineal gland and the pituitary gland, both marked out within the Great Pyramid, which is a giant replica of the third eye system.

The King's Chamber (pineal gland) vibrates at 8 hertz, as do the alpha waves of the human brain which become more activate and excitable when the pineal gland is awakened, and it also causes an altered state of consciousness. I will mention 432 hertz again in a little while. 432 hertz resonates with 8 hertz expanding consciousness and enabling you to tune into universal knowledge. The two hemispheres of the brain are synchronised with each other at 8 hertz and this harmony causes maximum flow of information. It is the key to activating full potential of the brain. 8 hertz also induces DNA replication, and that takes us back to the ankh which is, in itself, symbolising DNA duplication and replication, the key of life and the key to life. The neo-cortex of the brain, the 90%

unassigned, becomes awakened in this synchronisation and one then operates in all brain cell dendrites with the maximum information flow possible on that scale. It reawakens us to the orchestra of our thoughts.

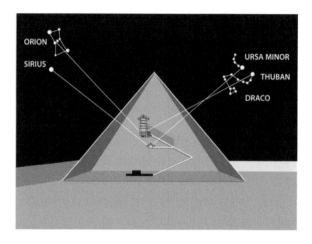

(Pyramid Shafts)

Even the much debated pyramid shafts were purposely directed at certain stars, and for good reason too. The pineal gland (King's Chamber) within the Great Pyramid has a shaft that faces Orion (also Osiris, known as the shaft of Osiris) and the pituitary gland (Isis/known as the Star Chamber of Isis) faces Sirius A (also Isis). This is, again, the two opposites, male and female facing South. The shafts are star chambers. Both the King's and Queen's Chambers were built rectangular, which symbolises stability. In the North (opposite of South facing shafts), we have two shafts facing Thuban in Ursa Minor and Draco. (The pineal gland is also known as the North Gate.) This is why the Great Pyramid is locked true north because the pineal gland is the North Gate.

Draco is now called the Dragon, however, in Ancient Egyptian times, it was called the Cobra/Serpent and it was one constellation. In higher dimensional terms, the serpent/dragon is symbolic of going beyond or leaving the solid world, shedding its skin, like the soul does as it leaves the physical skin, the body which can be done either living or otherwise.

The pyramid, the alchemical symbol of fire, at its two bottom corners represent the two opposites merging into one at the Apex, the Gold Cap stone (gold = symbolic of enlightenment), the Crown chakra. The pyramid base also represents the material/physical realm and the apex is a representation of the higher consciousness and transit from one to the other.

The third eye will only open when 'conscious fusion' takes place between the opposites of our own consciousness. There would have been various initiations and rituals within the pyramids to induce this state, accessed most probably through the guardian of higher knowledge, the Sphinx. It was the transition from unconscious matter to conscious existence with the mastery of this world and its duality, which is the symbolic meaning behind the legendary phoenix from the flames. They were reaching the mental state (Ment-Al = mind of God). The mind relates to the brain, the greater mind, the mental, relates to the higher consciousness state. So, in-keeping with theme of the balance of opposites, there are many Egyptian statues that are clearly holding onto two cylinder shaped metal rods, one in each hand. The foot position of these statues is also of relevance. When we see the left foot more prominently forward, it's of matriarchal significance, and when we see the right foot more prominently forward, it's symbolic of hermetic knowledge. But going back to the rods, these are what are known as the 'Wands of Horus', and they were metal cylinders filled with various special materials and quartz crystals of differing sizes to enhance their psychic and mental ability as well as the balancing of their chakras. This would bring harmony to their physical vessel and heal by regulating the energy balance of the body, and they were a tool for attainment and, unsurprisingly, enlightenment.

(The Wands of Horus - Copper held in right hand, Zinc held in the left)

All external and internal dimensions of the Wands of Horus conform strictly to the proportions of the golden section. This is of fundamental importance for the existence of resonant interaction between the cylinders and the user. To work effectively, the Wands of Horus need to attune themselves to the organism, while the user's organism, for its part, should also attune itself to the Wands of Horus. Such interaction is only possible when the cylinders conform to the proportions of the golden section, also known as the golden mean or golden ratio, which is connected to the Fibonacci numbers and the golden section in nature, art, geometry, architecture, music and even for calculating pi. The height of Wands of Horus is attuned to the pyramid and the diameter of the Wands is designed to be tuned to the Earth's 'eigenfrequency' which is a natural frequency, an inner frequency and a self-frequency. When we delve into ancient advanced knowledge of universe and self, we cannot but help stumbling across mathematics, sound, and frequencies. This is because the very fabric of existence is universal mathematical code.

The Wands of Horus take the form of two hollow cylinders made of copper and zinc for right and left hands respectively. This is important, because the link between metal and hand is tightly bound up with the functions of the left and right hemispheres of the brain. Copper was held in the right hand and this symbolised the Sun (male energy), and the zinc was held in the left hand and this symbolised the Moon (female energy), requiring the fundamental balance of the two.

Frequencies understood by the Egyptians were rediscovered by modern science with the Schuman frequency, also known as the Schumann Resonance Properties.

The spherical Earth-ionosphere cavity is created by the conductive surface of the Earth and the outer boundary of the ionosphere, separated by non-conducting air. Electromagnetic impulses are generated by electrical discharges such as lightning, the main excitation source, and spread laterally into the cavity. Lightning discharges have a "high-frequency component", involving frequencies between 1 kHz and 30 kHz, followed by a "low-frequency component" consisting of waves and frequencies below 2 kHz and gradually increasing amplitude. This produces electromagnetic waves in the very low frequency (VLF) and extremely low frequency (ELF) ranges. ELF waves at 3 Hz to 300 Hz are propagated as more or less strongly attenuated waves in the space between the Earth and the ionosphere, which provides a waveguide for the signals. Certain wavelengths circumnavigate the Earth with little attenuation. This is due to the fact that standing waves are formed within the cavity, the circumference of which is "approximately equal to the wavelength which an electromagnetic wave with a frequency of about 7.8 Hz would have in free space" (König, 1979, p34). It is the waves of this frequency and its harmonics at 14, 20, 26, 33, 39, and 45 Hz that form Schumann resonances.

Scientist Dr Ludwig came across the Ancient Chinese teachings which state that man needs two environmental signals: the YANG (masculine) signal from above and the YIN (feminine) signal from below. This description fits the relatively strong signal of the Schumann wave surrounding our planet being YANG and the weaker geomagnetic waves coming from below, from within the planet, being the YIN signal. This requires a balance of opposites and the balance of self, which was fully understood in Ancient Egypt. 432 hertz is the Godlike state, a perfect frequency, and when we use mathematics, we get from this number the formula 4+3+2 = 9, 432 hertz and hertz means the amount of oscillations per second. This frequency releases DMT from your pineal gland, which makes it easy to go straight into the avatar state. An avatar is a manifestation of a deity or released soul in bodily form on Earth, an incarnate divine teacher. DMT is a psychedelic serum within the brain, taking us into a spiritual mode. Chants at the right frequency help release Dimenthyltryptamine (DMT), which is a hallucinogenic drug that can be produced by the brain, especially during REM sleep.

The Egyptians used vowel-sounding chants to invoke certain reactions to enhance this practice. 432 HZ is a perfect balanced tone that helps you to grow metaphysically. The diameter of the moon is precisely 2160 miles, which is exactly 432 x 5. The diameter of the sun is 864.000 miles, which is 432.000 x 2. The number 432 is also found in the patterns of planet orbits. Pythagoras (570 - 495 BC) was a Greek philosopher, mathematician, astronomer, and scientist. He was credited for originating the "Music of the Spheres" theory, which states there are musical intervals (mathematical ratios) found in the distances and sizes of the planets and how they moved around one another. It gave name to the Pythagorean tuning scale, which turns out to produce the A=432 Hz! 432 is encoded into the very workings of the cosmos. Listening to the 432Hz frequency resonates inside our body, releases emotional blockages, and expands our consciousness. 432Hz is the 'Miracle Tone' and raises positive vibrations, being a healing frequency. 432 hertz is pitching 'A' on the musical scale. A = 432 Hz, known as Verdi's 'A', is an alternative tuning that is mathematically consistent with the universe. Music based on 432Hz transmits beneficial healing energy, because it is a pure tone of maths' fundamental connection to nature.

Verdi was a composer and it is said that the famous composers tuned their music and symphonies to this tone and frequency also. The letter 'A' is also the pyramid shape and would resonate with the same tone and frequency. Archaic Egyptian instruments that have been unearthed are largely tuned to A=432 Hz. 432 Hz unites you with the universal harmony. This tone is closely related to the universe around us, it is the pitch of energy release, chakra tuning, relaxation and meditation, and healing. 432 hertz is enlightened consciousness. Ancient Egyptian instruments, such as the sistra or sistrum, are tuned to this frequency and its importance can be seen in many carvings and hieroglyphs shown in the Temples of Egypt.

432 is a sacred universal number that other cultures have harnessed too. For example, at the Buddhist Borobudur Temple in Indonesia, there are 432 statues of Buddha, which is an esoteric reference to this number. Even Tibetan singing bowls are set at this frequency. The lotus flower is significant in these cultures

as well as in Egypt where, in addition to enlightenment, the Egyptians also saw it as the joining of Lower and Upper Egypt due to its intertwining stems. We have been left a wonderful advanced knowledge by our ancient ancestors and, as the full picture reveals itself piece by piece, I sit here in wonderment. The pyramids represent consciousness and how to reach it. Not only was one of the pyramid shafts facing Orion/Osiris to show us the connection to the pineal gland (also relevant to the King's Chamber), but also the three main pyramids of Giza are aligned to the constellation of Orion too, to reinforce this message.

Many scholars have correctly identified the advanced mathematics within the pyramids that make up their dimensions and structure but what they have missed are their pinnacle purpose, which are their numerical frequencies of consciousness and how to invoke consciousness. It is true that we can find advanced mathematics within them, but they are not simply mathematics, which is a fact these scholars have also seemingly missed. These mathematical numbers are there not only for design and structural building diameters, but also for the consciousness frequencies of the numbers themselves, for example, 3.14159 which is pi. Pi vibrates at 528 hertz, which is known as the miracle tone, restoring consciousness to full potential, and 528 hertz is a frequency that is central to the musical mathematical matrix of creation. Amazingly, within the numerical digits of pi, there is encoded the states of the brain within the numerical digits themselves and also the atomic co-ordinates of the human atomic and genetic code. Pi is a transcendental number, meaning it deals with the spirit realm and gives us quantum immortality.

There are other famous number sequences too, such as the golden mean/ratio and, of course, the Fibonacci sequence which we are told by the history books was discovered by Leonardo De Pisa in

1202, this is not correct as it was used in the Egyptian pyramids. Nevertheless, the golden ratio and the Fibonacci sequence both have a frequency of 432 hertz, which I have already discussed in terms of extreme relevance and also the balance of the third dimension.

When we tune into universal knowledge and information, everything that has previously been stored and input there can be used and accessed by others of that race. It is a morphogenetic grid of sorts. I think that the Egyptians and others used this method in the construction of their monuments and the secret and sacred knowledge that they encoded within them, hiding in a secret place the knowledge of what they truly represent. And their two main gods are really metaphors for the pineal and pituitary glands, Osiris and Isis.

Pineal gland definition:

The pineal gland, conarium, or epiphysis cerebri, is a small endocrine gland in the brain of most vertebrates. The pineal gland produces melatonin, a serotonin-derived hormone which modulates sleep patterns in both circadian and seasonal cycles. The shape of the gland resembles a pine cone from which it derived its name. The pineal gland is located in the epithalamus, near the centre of the brain, between the two hemispheres, tucked in a groove where the two halves of the thalamus join. The pineal gland is one of the neuroendocrine secretory circumventricular organs that are not part of the blood-brain-barrier. Epiphysis gives us the Christian celebration of epiphany.

Pituitary gland definition:

In vertebrate anatomy, the pituitary gland, or hypophysis, is an endocrine gland about the size of a pea and weighing 0.5 grams in humans. It is a protrusion off the bottom of the hypothalamus at the base of the brain. The hypophysis rests upon the hypophysial fossa of the sphenoid bone in the centre of the middle cranial fossa and is surrounded by a small bony cavity covered by a dural fold. The anterior pituitary is a lobe of the gland that regulates several physiological processes. The intermediate lobe synthesizes and secretes melanocyte-stimulating hormone. The posterior pituitary is a lobe of the gland that is functionally connected to the hypothalamus by the median eminence via a small tube called the pituitary stalk.

Both the pineal gland and the pituitary gland form the endocrine system of the brain, the third eye of spiritual sight. 'Endocrine' means 'secretion within' and that secretion, which comes from the pineal gland, is a brown and white substance. This brown and white substance is the biblical land of '*Milk and Honey*'.

The pineal gland and the pituitary gland is Osiris and Isis, and this is the chemical marriage of opposites, or 'tying the knot', a term also used in modern day marriages.

The marriage of Osiris and Isis may be represented by the numerical proportion of 6/5. In terms of musical intervals, 6/5 is a minor third. A symmetrical scale comprised solely of minor thirds is called a 'diminished scale', and divides the octave into 4 equal minor third intervals. If one places the 12 semitones of an octave around a circle and then draws straight lines to connect the notes of a diminished scale to one another (in the pictorial example given later on, the scale consists of the notes C, Eb/D#, Gb/F#, and A), the lines form a square. The minor third, 6 and 5, Osiris and Isis, all square the circle.

"I see 6/5 more as a resonance built into the architecture of the universe" – Scott Onstott

5 and 6, which also gives us the number 11, the conveyer of divine light, gives us Adam and Eve and Isis and Osiris, as you will see. This mathematical formula is also hidden within the Red and Bent Pyramids of Dashur (Egypt), which represent the pentagram and hexagram (numbers 5+6).

"He who joins the hexagram and pentagram has solved half of the sacred secret" –Eliphas Levi (19th-century magician)

Squaring the circle has been a mathematical problem for hundreds of years, however, unbeknown to many, you can square the circle musically using the numbers 5 and 6 - the pentagram and the hexagram.

And this is how:

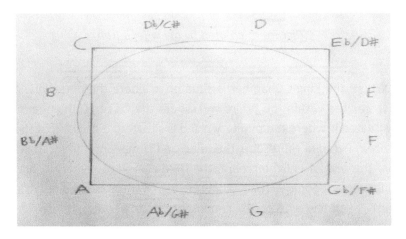

(Pictorial Example of Osiris and Isis Musically Squaring the Circle)

Osiris and Isis (pineal gland and pituitary gland) also feature in the Great Pyramid in a clandestine way. What gets interesting from this point is if you, and I have, place an overlay of the human head over the Great Pyramid, facing north, for reasons already stated, you get this:

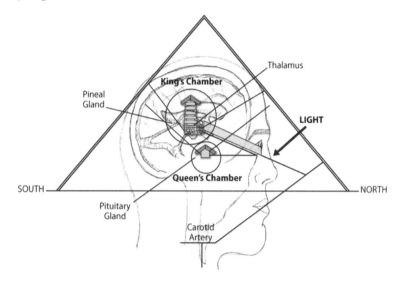

(Picture re-created by my wife, Sarah)

Where the King's Chamber is situated is where the pineal gland is situated within the brain, and where the Queen's Chamber is situated is where the pituitary gland is situated. It shows that the Great Pyramid represents the mind and is marking the locations of the seat of enlightenment, the third eye. Pretty amazing, and not many people actually know this, you are now amongst the privileged few who do. I will mention the tower in a little while. There are three chambers in the Great Pyramid and the three degrees of the ancient mysteries were, with few exceptions, given in chambers which represented the three great centres of the human and universal bodies. If possible, the temple itself was constructed in the form of the human body. The candidate entered between the feet and received the highest degree in the point corresponding to the brain. The first degree was the material mystery and its symbol was the generative system.

It raised the candidate through the various degrees of concrete thought. The second degree was given in the chamber corresponding to the heart, but represented the middle power which was the mental link. Here, the candidate was initiated into the mysteries of abstract thought and lifted as high as the mind was capable of penetrating. He then passed into the third chamber, which, analogous to the brain, occupied the highest position in the temple but, analogous to the heart, was of the greatest dignity. In the brain chamber, the heart mystery was given. Here the initiate, for the first time, truly comprehended the meaning of those immortal words: *"As a man thinketh in his heart, so is he"*.

I saw a recent documentary in which many scholars were scratching their heads as to the meaning of the Great Pyramid's subterranean chambers. Let me tell you now.

The subterranean chambers represent the subconscious mind, the unconscious levels of the mind (darkness). The need is to utilise the power of Daath (knowledge in the Kabballah) to awaken our eyes. The subconscious mind can be a place of illusion, good or bad. Without the removal of ego, we become a diviner/seer who sees through the filter of 'I', which is ego, and this is the creation of a demon. This is illustrated by the path of RA through the underworld, because the alchemist makes his descent into the underworld of his soul to recover the treasure buried in matter in order to birth a new transformed consciousness. What he then finds is the transmutation of the mind called in the Bible, in Matthew 6:19-24, *"the treasure of heaven"* (heaven being the mind) and this treasure is enlightenment (alchemical gold).

This is also the meaning behind the famous heads of Easter Island which represent the Herma, the divine mind, or the square/ rectangular stone, also known as the philosopher's stone. Herma gives us Hermes, who takes us to the Gods and out of the lower worlds. In Greek, 'Herma' means 'square/rectangular stone', and it represents the head of divinity.

(Herma)

The primordial Adam comes out of the stone; he who is perfected, sculpted, and crafted out of the philosophical stone, the philosophical Earth. By detaching oneself from the body consciousness and by controlling the mind (fixing the mind on the higher self) you attain enlightenment, 'Moai' means 'to listen', and that is how the pineal gland receives. The philosophical stone is the intimate Christ, the heavenly fire within us, our profound innermost saviour. It is the stages of development and the power over nature. Below the ground on the Easter Island statues, their hands point at their naval because the naval is the centre of internal alchemy, where you can unify body, mind, and spirit. They are 33 feet high, which has spiritual significance, as mentioned in the Jesus chapter, and all heads face east which, in cardinal points, is the direction of illumination and enlightenment. This is why the Sphinx and Egyptian mummies also face east. East is where the sun rises. There are believed to be 1000 heads, and 1000 is also spiritually significant, this is why there are 1000 petals on the lotus flower upon the head of Buddha. The gigantic heads were also energy emitters of 'Negative Green', which facilitate resonance with higher realms. They are radio waves that carry sound information.

Within Masonry, the herma is the masonic stone representing the knowledge contained in the stone, Hermes' symbol of and patron of knowledge. It is the perfect cube (philosopher's stone). In Islam, in their sacred place, we have Mecca, and 'Mecca' means 'cube'. It is within 'Kaaba', which means 'square house'. It is walked around 7 times, which is really the 7 stages of alchemical magnum opus, the great work. When you amalgamate Kaaba with the Islamic God Allah, you get Kaaba-Allah, which is the Kabballah. *"Masonry, like all the religions and all the mysteries, hermeticism and alchemy, conceals its secrets from all but the adepts and the sages (sage derives from Saggitarius which is the symbol of philosophy) or the elect. And it uses false explanations and misinterpretations of its symbols to mislead those who deserve only to be misled, to conceal the truth, which it calls light, from them ad to draw them away from it"* – Manly P Hall.

The tower-looking structure within the Great Pyramid is known in the mainstream as 'relief chambers'. But they, of course, have an esoteric meaning. They are what are replicated in Japan and China by the Shinto temple. 'Shinto' gives us 'Shen' which means 'Gods', and 'Tao' which means 'path' or 'way'. Therefore, it is a pathway to the Gods.

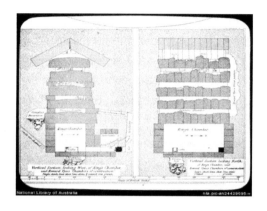

(Tower with the Great Pyramid and a Shinto tower in Japan)

In essence, three of the main Gods of Egypt - Osiris, Isis, and Horus - are representations of the three parts of the third eye; the pineal gland (Osiris), pituitary gland (Isis), and the thalamus (Horus).

The pyramid shafts that face various star systems are capturing star frequencies and the likes of Sirius; a 33rd degree initiation frequency, which is why it features heavily in Masonry as the 'Blazing Star'. Sirius is associated with the Goddess Isis, who is associated with the Mayan Queen Moo (Mu). Moo (Mu) is code for the emanation of the light of Sirius and this is the fabled land of

Lemuria, therefore Lemuria is the pituitary gland. I will talk about Atlantis later. The word 'Sirius' means 'scorching'. This is also true of the mathematical sequences within the pyramid too, such as the Fibonacci sequence, golden mean/ration, and pi, which all have consciousness raising frequencies. Even Disney movies and Walt Disney was a 33rd degree mason, and even Pinocchio has Sirius relevance. Pinocchio means 'pine-eye', which is the pineal gland, the haze of the blue fairy is the light of Sirius, and Sirius is a star of luck, hence the famous song *'Wish Upon A Star'*. Pinocchio wanting to be a boy also has connections to initiations. Pinocchio turning into a donkey is symbolic of degenerating into an animalistic nature. Sirius 'A', known as the Sun behind the Sun, is the 33rd degree ascension frequency of masonry (33 degrees) and its blue haze gives us the blue lodges. Man arrives at Sirius as the perfected human being.

The Number 153:

The number 153 will feature again later with the identity of Mary Magdalene, the bride of Christ, which also has significant relevance to Christ too, detailed in a later chapter of this book. Please remember this section of this chapter when you arrive there regarding the number 153, which gives us 1+5=3=9 completion and esoteric man.

153 is the number of sacred knowledge, and is intrinsically written in the Great Pyramid. The entrance to the Great Pyramid, which has above it a double chevron meaning 'Chibur', 'the place of connection', a connection between the material and the spiritual worlds, is on the seventeenth course level. This is important, because if we add up all of the numbers from 1-17, as such 1+2+3+4+5+6+7+8+9+10+11+12+13+14+15+16+17, it equals

153.

It is a world within a world mirror (Halls of Amenti/Hall of Mirrors) with a gateway in and out using numbers as crossing angles of reality hotspots where the spiritual and material meet up (Chibur). This system is guarded by an advanced encryption system by numbers but also by intentions.

The Grand Gallery of the Great Pyramid is 153 feet long and has 153 steps. The Great Pyramid is 480.69 feet high which, when divided by 153, gives us the mathematical pi. Pi corresponds to 528 hertz, which is a consciousness raising frequency. 153 is the 17th triangular number and 17 is the entrance level of this pyramid and, by using this mathematical formula of 17 x 9 (entrance level plus the number of pyramids), you get 153.

Consciousness was pinnacle to the Egyptian secret.

(King Tutankhamun's Death Mask)

The death mask of King Tutankhamun shows us various aspects of consciousness. The cobra's spread hood is the cerebellum of the brain separated by the vermis, meaning 'serpent'. The beard-looking aspect is the sex force that has lifted and enlivened all occult centres of the brain. The gold is the colour of completion of Magnum Opus, the Great Work of alchemy. The black eyeliner is a symbol of Osiris, the third eye (pineal gland), and the earrings demonstrate a masculine and feminine union.

Not only does the human body have meridians and energy centres, but so does the land. When you look at the African Prime Meridian, you can see that Giza is situated in the position of the third eye and Alexandria in the position of the crown chakra.

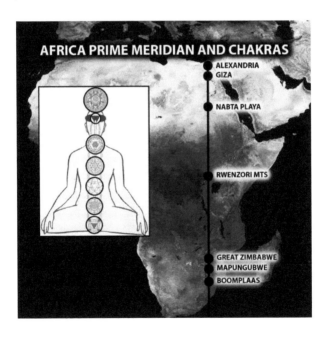

(Africa Prime Meridians)

Ancient sites, such as Stonehenge, were also resonance chambers to induce consciousness, transmute DNA, and transmute their beings. The pyramids, and the Great Pyramid in particular, was an amplification and resonance chamber for such transformation through sound alchemy. That now leads me onto the elongated skulls mystery. Elongated skulls have not only been found in Egypt but also Stonehenge, Peru, and Arkaim, which is known as Russia's Stonehenge. Many have theorised that they are extra-terrestrial skulls with non-earthly DNA, but what are they? Here's my take on the mystery.

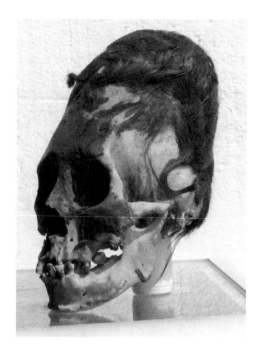

(Elongated Skull)

The shafts at the top of the Great Pyramid were designed as receivers of the lowest frequencies of intrasound, 0.5 hertz, which is sound inaudible to the human ear. Loud intrasound has a wave between 0.5 – 10 hertz.

This was at the precise place of the shaft affecting the transmission of sound waves. The airshafts were harmonic dimensions that specify wavelengths and storing soundwaves. This created an acoustic resonance system, also known as psycho-acoustic, for genetic enhancement and consciousness balancing. They would place babies into the shafts at the location that they open up into the upper chamber.

(One of the small shafts)

This process was also conducted within the womb with a process called cranial augmentation, which is fetal gestation and natal biorhythmic entrainment, basically changing the shape of the skull. This would then create infrasonic stimulation causing genetic enhancement, which is why science finds what it considers to be non-human DNA; it is really transmuted DNA. The shafts were DNA and nativity chambers for connecting and stabilising the biorhythms of mother and child at separation at birth. The Egyptians were using gestational entrainment techniques under the Great Pyramid's magnetic umbrella. The dimensions of the sarcophagus are calibrated to the heartbeat of a new-born child.

(Sarcophagus)

The left hand corner of the sarcophagus has stone missing. Egyptologists tell you that it has been broken, but it has not been broken at all. This was to allow liquid to leave for, what I think is, a much earlier practise of the Hebrew mikvah bath, which was to recreate the womb experience (mentioned in more detail in the Noah chapter).

Cones have a dynamic sonic effect and an enhanced spectrum in the frequency dimension, therefore the elongated skulls was a sound-induced enhancement of DNA. I would also say that sound, which has levitation properties, enabled the large and heavy stones of ancient monuments to be lifted, and sound at an even higher frequency creates a laser beam, which is how I would suggest the stones were cut with laser precision all around the world, to such an extent that a thin piece of paper cannot fit between the stones themselves. A team of researchers in Switzerland have developed a way of levitating and transporting objects using nothing but sound. Using ultrasonic waves that is, sound waves whose frequencies are too high for humans to hear, scientists at the Swiss Federal Institute of Technology in Zurich have made water droplets, instant coffee crystals, Styrofoam flakes, and a toothpick, among other objects, hang in mid-air, move along a plane, and interact with each other. It is the first time that scientists have been able to use sound to simultaneously levitate several objects next to each other and move them around. But it isn't the first time, in my opinion; the Egyptians did it many thousands of years ago.

In 2010, researchers built sound lasers, coaxing a collection of phonons to travel together. But those first devices were hybrid models that used the light from a traditional laser to create a coherent sound emission. In traditional lasers, a bunch of electrons in a gas or crystal are excited all at the same time. When they relax back to their lower energy state, they release a specific wavelength of light, which is then directed with mirrors to produce a beam. Sound lasers work on a similar principle. A mechanical oscillator jiggles and excites a bunch of phonons, which relax and release their energy back into the device. The confined energy causes the phasor to vibrate at its fundamental frequency but with at a very narrow wavelength. The sound laser produces phonons at 170 kilohertz, far above human hearing range, which peters out around 20 kilohertz. The pyramids were resonance chambers.

Egypt was a sacred land of enlightenment. Their pyramids marked the completion of the Magnum Opus of alchemy and the Great Pyramid maps out the location within the brain of the third eye, therefore being a gigantic representation of the mind. Their culture was to create a higher type of human. They knew that sexual energy used for the beast (spasm of the animal – orgasm) will prevent the human being. It is our Eros which is erotic nature, the order out of chaos, chaos followed by order during penetration. It is the fire that unites all things. Only by man and women can life be created. They knew that a higher consciousness, included transcending animal instinct, illustrated by the Sphinx. In Egyptian mythology, their God, Osiris, was severed into 14 different pieces, with the only part of him unable to be located being the phallus, illustrated by the obelisk and even the church spire. This is telling us of the resurrected master without lust; in other words, the master who has overcome his lower animal instinct and desires. The famous solar boat symbolises enlightenment, whereby only the enlightened can illuminate the seat, the seat being the throne of the eye, the pineal gland. It is the boat of higher self. We must pass through the Halls of Amenti, the hall of mirrors, the illusion, only passable through knowledge and wisdom.

Another hidden message of consciousness is given to us in the Egyptian God Thoth, which is really 'thought'. Thought is intransitive awareness without form, seen in many Egyptian depictions as Thoth travelling with a baboon. It is the secret fire at its highest sense. The baboon is the olfactory tract within the brain that, when opened up, resembles a monkey.

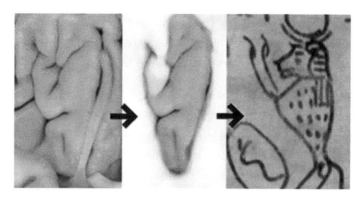

(The Olfactory Tract)

The Olfactory Tract is our nervous system communication

network and a sensory way of communicating to a higher place, taking us from our Lower Egypt (lower body) to our Upper Egypt (higher body) which meet at the brain. As my revelations about the ancient code has always stated, there is a deep connection between ancient cultures who were telling us the same hidden coded message.

American Indians for example didn't cut their hair as it is a nervous system connection from Earth to heaven, between the body and the stars and hairs are natural antennas. The nervous system is controlled by the Olfactory tract of the brain which when opened out resembles a baboon. The baboon with Thoth is really referring to olfactory consciousness.

Thoth is code for thought which is the secret fire at its highest sense. Thought is energy and energy is matter, therefore thought is and can be a physical manifestation!

(Thoth 'thought', on the boat)

The boat is symbolic of the brainwaves travelling along the cerebrospinal fluid to reach and communicate with each aspect of the body.

How consciousness is generated by the nervous system remains one of the greatest mysteries in science. Investigators from diverse fields have begun to unravel this puzzle by contrasting conscious and unconscious processes. Olfaction, perhaps the phylogenetically oldest sensory modality (Hosek and Freeman, 2001), is unique among sensory modalities in its anatomical organization (Price, 1990, Freeman, 2007a). Most notably, unlike other sensory modalities (e.g, vision, audition, or touch), bottom-up afference from the olfactory receptors bypasses the thalamic "first-order" relay neurons (Sherman and Guillery, 2006) and directly influences a region of the ipsilateral cortex (Shepherd and Greer, 1998,Tham et al, 2009), called the olfactory (piriform) cortex (Haberly, 1998, Mori et al, 1999, Neville and Haberly, 2004, Gottfried and Zald, 2005). Specifically, after sensory transduction in the olfactory epithelium of the nose, olfactory afference undergoes sophisticated processing in the olfactory bulb, a structure that can generate complex patterns of activation across neural populations, which are used for the encoding of odorants (Freeman, 1987, Xu et al., 2000).

While historically the olfactory bulb was compared to the retina (Ramón y Cajal, 1909–1911), it has been proposed more recently that the primary function carried out by the bulb is similar to the primary function carried out by the first-order relay thalamus (e.g, the lateral geniculate nucleus) in other sensory modalities (e.., vision): "both structures act as a bottleneck that is a target for various modulatory inputs, and this arrangement enables efficient control of information flow before cortical processing occurs" (Kay and Sherman, 2007, p. 47).

After processing in the bulb, olfactory afference is processed in the piriform (meaning, "pear-shaped") cortex. The piriform cortex is considered to be part of the "primary olfactory cortex," which also includes the olfactory tubercle, the periamygdaloid cortex, the lateral entorhinal cortex, the cortical portion of the amygdaloid nuclei, the ventral tenia teat, and the nucleus of the lateral olfactory tract (Carmichael et al, 1994, Tham et al., 2009). Piriform cortex is a phylogenetically old type of cortex, hence the namesake of this kind of cortex, paleocortex. Paleocortex contains only three cortical layers, which stands in contrast to neocortex, which contains six layers. (It is worth noting that the analogous cortical regions for the modalities of vision and audition consist, not of paleocortex, but of neocortex.) Interestingly, though paleocortex is less complex than neocortex, it still shares remarkable similarities with the neocortex, in terms of physiology, neurochemistry, and local circuitry (Haberly, 1998). Thus, by studying this possibly more simple form of cortex, one can learn a great deal about neocortex.

Despite the relative simplicity of the piriform cortex, it has been suggested that the anatomical connectivity of the posterior piriform may allow it to perform complex operations such as learning, memory retrieval, and other associative functions (Haberly, 1998).

It is clear that the olfactory system is well suited system for the isolation of a neural correlate of consciousness. There are phenomenological and cognitive/mechanistic properties that render the olfactory system a fruitful network in which to investigate the contrast between conscious and unconscious processing. But of course the Egyptians knew this many thousands of years ago.

I was recently asked why such a sacred land had disappeared and I replied that it hasn't, it has been hidden. The symbology of Egypt is very much alive - in pop culture, in politics, in secret societies, or should I say societies with secrets, in royalty and in religions, in fact, its secrets are everywhere. A day does not pass without seeing numerous Egyptian symbols.

Egypt was the land of the higher type of human. And how did they lift gigantic stones and cut them with laser precision? By sound! At certain frequencies, the stones were lifted and, at an even higher frequency, a laser beam is produced, cutting the stones with perfection!

Egypt is also engrained into modern society, especially the likes of America, Paris, and London. Some examples of this are the Obelisk and Glass Pyramid in central Paris, Big Ben which is the Benebenet, the pyramid capstone, situated at the Houses of Parliament and the river Thames deriving from 'Tamas' meaning 'dark river', now representing Apophis, the opposer of light, which was formerly known as Isis, the river Goddess; all of which are situated in central London.

The seat motifs within the House of Commons are the Hoshen, which was the breast plate of the Serpent Priests of Osiris (Djedhi). The Djedhi, the Serpent Priests (Serpent representing Wisdom) and initiates of the Ancient Mystery Schools of Egypt were the protectors of the Temple of Osiris, indicated by the Djed (spine of Osiris symbolising strength). They later became the Druids of the British Isles; 'Druid' meaning 'Oak Knowledge' (tree knowledge). The Djed is the spine (Jacob's Ladder) and, at the top of the spine is the head, the Temple, which means 'House of God' and 'house' means 'mind'! So, in other words, the Djedhi (Jedi for you *Star Wars* fans) were the protectors of the sacred knowledge of consciousness which they brought to Britain from Egypt. And, of course, the river Thames itself is Apophis the dark serpent who caused famine in Egypt by swallowing the water of the Nile. His head is where the O2 arena is now situated (02 = Oxygen). Apophis is the opposer of light and the enemy of Isis. Even the three City of London police stations are set out to the shape of the constellation of Orion's belt (Orion is associated with Osiris). In this region, we have Hyde Park with derives from Hydra, the serpent, which is the name of the river within Hyde Park.

Then we get to America ('Ameruca', which means 'land of the feathered serpent') which is rife with Egyptian symbology and meaning. The Declaration of Independence signed on the 4th July was significant by virtue of the fact that, on 4th July, Sirius 'A' is furthest away from the solar Sun and the Founding Fathers wished to commemorate this invisibility into their history. It was signed in Philadelphia; Philae is where the temple of Isis is situated in Egypt, and 'Delphi' means 'Delphos' which is the womb. Isis is the Goddess of motherhood, and this is also signified by the dome-shaped buildings in the likes of Washington DC (District of Columbia, Columbia is a form of Isis) and, of course, the Obelisk, the corner stone of which was erected at the exact time Sirius 'A' passed overhead at precisely 10:59am on August 7th 1880.

The Church of Philadelphia is code for the pineal gland. The Statue of Liberty, which was originally destined for Egypt, from where the enlightenment of the world will emanate, is Isis and her flame is Horus; these characters are Semiramis and Nimrod in Babylon. But, nevertheless, it represents the masonic enlightenment of the world, hence the 7 rays from Liberty's head. which are symbolic of the enlightened mind. It is Sirius 'A' and the solar Sun. The ancient capital of Egypt was Memphis, which means 'White Walls', and this is why America has a White House! Within the White House, there is the 'Oval Office', again, referring to the womb and fertility of Isis. Even the good old hotdog is Egyptian. In July and August, the Sun was so hot that the Egyptians would try and appease the heat. They believed that Sirius 'A' gave the Sun its power and therefore they would sacrifice a dog to Sirius (the dog star) called 'dog days'. The hotdog is symbolic of this canine ritual sacrifice.

The Egyptians knew, and understood, the workings of our most inner-self, and they practiced wholeness and divinity, reaching the dizzy heights of enlightenment. They knew how to find and extract knowledge and wisdom from their own DNA/RNA that we can only do now by way of sophisticated and advanced technical scientific equipment, that we are told is a product of the 21st century.

There were 3 main pyramids at Giza; The Great pyramid, which is Khufu's pyramid (Khufu means 'Name of a Pharaoh', and in numerology this name has an expression/core number of 22, which is the number I continue to frequently see), Khafre's pyramid (Khafre is a variant of Khufu), and Menkaure's pyramid ('Menkaure' means 'Divine'). The Egyptians had a quadrant system of consciousness which were as follows: they were Osiris, Isis, and Horus as the pineal gland, pituitary gland, and the Thalamus and the Cerebellum, situated as part of the endocrine system of the human brain.

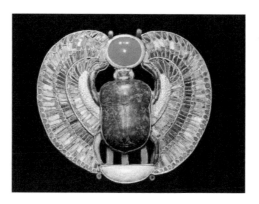

(The Scarab Beetle depicting wings of the Cerebellum)

The scarab beetle also represents the lateral wings of the Cerebellum, the hemispheres, and the Aten, the Inner Sun/ Light. Wings can also mean a hidden potential to vanquish base characteristics (depravity) and shows of mans capacity to rise above and master his potential. An example of this is a church Gargoyle which is a vivid reminder of this and symbolises that the state in which man lives does not dictate his divinity.

Giza, meaning 'border', representing Upper and Lower Egypt, North and South of the Nile Delta, were merged by the Mind – Memphis, the symbolic Mind, with Heliopolis being the Heart and Thebes being the Tongue; HTM - Heart, Tongue and Mind. Upper and Lower Egypt also represent the lower and upper body, and higher and lower consciousness within us. Memphis was the original capital city. And, in line with frequencies, the Great Pyramids of Giza harness the very sound waves from the inner core of the Earth which coincides with alpha; the rhythms produced by the human brain during meditation. The pyramids, Earth, and the brain have the same range of frequencies. This is an advanced knowledge of sound/vibrational frequencies.

THE ANKH:

The Ankh, the key of life, is really the process of DNA and protein synthesis. Protein synthesis is the biological generation of cells that bind with DNA. When protein binds with DNA, it loops and crosses around and over it and bonds in loop shapes before closing itself and tying itself off, which is symbolised in the ankh shape. The ankh, key of life, is referring to DNA. Life DNA synthesis is the expansion and creation through the double helix DNA system of reproduction and revitalising of genetics which, again, is essential within the term life.

(Egyptian Ankh and DNA Synthesis)

Everything in creation is a smaller version of the larger, the microcosm, macrocosm Russian doll effect and whereas the human body has an energy meridian system, so do countries and so do planets; they all have meridian leylines.

The Egyptians and others, through and with their magnificent monuments, were showing us the anatomy of the human brain, a gigantic replica of our Endocrine third eye system of consciousness, and how to achieve divinity and cosmic consciousness by the balancing of opposites at the apex. Indicated by the Golden Pyramid capstone, where duality becomes whole, it becomes one, we have mastered the physical world, with each chakra having first been balanced. This was so large that its importance could be in no doubt. They wanted to show us how much it meant to them and what value had been placed upon it, a massive statement in the desert. And it isn't only pyramids, many churches and cathedrals are also showing the endocrine system when you overlay a figure of the human head over their floor plans too.

We have been left, in the most grand and significant way, the key and path to enlightenment by an advanced race that knew the secrets of body and universe, and its connections. Maybe we can follow them into greatness! Consciousness was everything to the hierarchy of Egyptian society and all that they did was work towards the God-state.

The Great Pyramid is the human brain's consciousness functions, the mathematics of the pyramids are numeric consciousness frequencies, and balance is the way of attaining Christ consciousness. We are being told, in the most wondrous of ways, and all we need do is listen and hear!

There are many monuments all around the world that are aligned to the constellation of Orion and this is for the exact same reason; consciousness and its connection to the pineal gland. This proves that these ancient cultures were tapping into the same knowledge base.

FIVE

STONEHENGE:
THE GIANT ENIGMA MACHINE

My wife and I visited Stonehenge in 2009 and heard the many versions of their purpose and their builders. From the Druids to Merlin, through a race of giants, who dropped the stones used to build the Stonehenge during a transit between two places across Salisbury Plain. But, despite the efforts of the mainstream, there seemed to me, as always, a greater purpose and a deeper mystery, and I have discovered that there indeed is. So, in fine tradition of my research and work, please join me for some revelations. I also went to Stonehenge in March 2019 when I took a group on an esoteric inner circle tour and it was a magnificent day where we made the stones sing, literally.

In ancient times certain cultures would align the population using precognition (gathering of knowledge) to form one mind and one accord (harmony). Starting at the centre of our galaxy, Orion, then the centre of the 12 constellations (Zodiac) then the planets at certain times/dates/months and time calendar on specific earth locations (usually leylines). Even down to the city and building layout. It would be embedded to encode a subliminal message into the subconscious mind and even DNA. The secret they were trying to teach us was how to change one from the other through induction using certain higher dimensional spiritual laws that govern the universe and how to connect to this other matrix world that we cannot see. Orion was so important to many cultures who aligned their monuments to its belt. This harmonic consciousness is one reason so many ancient sites were aligned to Orion, but there are of course other reasons which sre detailed in this book.

Salisbury:

Stonehenge is a world famous set of monoliths on the plains of Salisbury. Many have tried to guess their purpose. I hope today will answer many questions for you and put the whole ancient world into some perspective; their advanced knowledge and their unquestionable connection to people from the stars and, in the case of Stonehenge and Silbury Hill, Planet Mars in particular, as you will later see.

Stonehenge is, in effect, a gigantic phonetic profiler, capable of deciphering messages within soundwaves that contains a language, messages from other worlds, that allow the wise and in-tune masters of sound to add to their wisdom. It was a large tuning fork to balance and purify their own vessel to a pitch of a higher place. There are coded messages within soundwaves which are being decoded by an ancient enigma machine. Messages can also be transferred within light, and Alexander Graham Bell proved this to be the case with his Photophone whereby the voice was projected through an instrument toward the back of a mirror, which would oscillate when the vibrations from the voice hit it.

Sunlight was directed at the mirror, which captured those oscillations and projected them to a receiving mirror, at which point the oscillations were turned back into sound.

This is in the same vein as the modern SETI (Search for Extra-terrestrial Intelligence) that we use today, sending out messages within radio waves in the hope that they will reach a far and distant race. Well, they have already been here and most probably still are.

Through the use of various sonic techniques by using crystalline monoliths as harmonic tuning forks and ancient computers as we use silicon in computers today, they were able to transcend to other worlds and ascend their own vessels to God-state highness.

The advanced science and knowledge of ancient times is returning.

AT THE BEGINNING: THE MASTERS OF FREQUENCY

Imagine landing on Earth, and looking for and finding suitable locations around the planet to build communications systems back to your own planet.

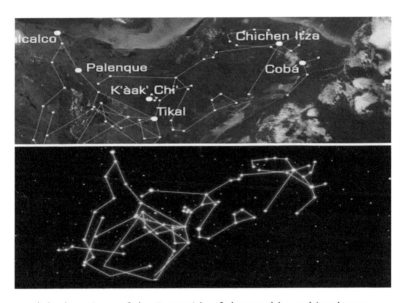

(The locations of the Pyramids of the world combined are a star-map)

The Earthly monuments are energy directors, and the stones themselves were moved by 'sound wave focusing'. They are sound wave constructions.

The correlations of the rocks were a power source energised by electromagnetic fields, built upon magnetic energy focus points, leylines. You can modify wavelengths to carry sound information and add information to a frequency wavelength. Something as simple as a piece of glass can change an electromagnetic wavelength, which is called the 'Index of Refraction'. Bear in mind that many extra-terrestrial languages are frequency based.

Consciousness and balance within was important because, at the centre of within, we can create high melodic sounds brought forth whilst in a trance state. Stonehenge was an energy transducer, which is a device that converts energy from one form to another or converts a signal in one form of energy to a signal in another.

The location attracted those on the correct frequency who, in turn, placed stones in the correct location to receive the coded communications in code telepathy. This code could also be found in encoded pictographs.

(Nazca Lines = Encoded Communications)

This is as a result of focused transcendent thought wave separation. Many messages are in spiral form as the spiral serves to translate a message by slowing down the wave and focusing thought wave transference energy that also moves in spirals.

This utilises/transduces electromagnetic waves, which is the conduit for breaking down a signal from universal languages into a phonetic profile. Phonetic profiling is transcribing sounds that occur in a language; letters that represent sounds. It is like a gigantic WWII 'Enigma Code Breaking Machine'. This was for the purpose of multiple user necessity.

Therefore, multiple people must hear, feel, and understand the same thing.

Stonehenge was used to resonate with the 'tonal rill', which taught wise ones with wisdoms entered physically through the crown chakra transceiving system (transmitter/receiver system of circuitry).

This happens to me too, and I can feel the information/ancient knowledge being entered into my mind but without any need for these rituals and without summons.

Tonal rill is a download through overtone singing. Overtone is a single human voice simultaneously producing two or more clearly audible tones (Tones = stones/ ringtones = ringstones) which can then be caused to harmonise with the self. The human voice is able to interact with the stones by using a special vocal technique, creating a distinctive ringing sound by isolating only particular harmonics. It is a precise resonant frequency of the stone, therefore vibrating it.

Rill is a breathy sound made by forcing air through the space between the tip of the tongue and the roof of the mouth which can levitate stone.

Sound and light are intertwined with one another and both carry information; the root word of Sun/son is 'sonic'. All ancient sites have information stored in the stone as the human body has information stored in its bones. When sound moves through you, it unlocks a doorway and allows an information flood into your body. It also penetrates into the ground, affecting Earth vibrations and changing molecular alignment.

Crystalline structures can transmit a large amount of information to evolved/plugged-in humans.

Sound is a tool for transformation for the keepers of sound. Stonehenge is circular because it can open a columnar portal at the circle's centre, creating circular waves. Circular resonance can create portals. Overtones also activate the inner portal, the pineal gland.

The stones were a chakra balancer and an amplification of the transmitter and receiver energies, connecting Earth and sky.

The Presli bluestones of Stonehenge have 7 bands of energy that connect to the 7 chakras.

The whole area of this region, which also contains Stonehenge itself, was believed to have spanned over several miles. Originally, 700 stones may have been present in various locations within that region, which looks different today from what it did then. The number 700 is very apt as it represents the evolution of the microcosm, the seven principles of the man. It is the symbol of the resurrection as an image of the phoenix, this mythological bird that once burnt and reappeared out of its own ashes. In Greek, the numerical value of phoenix, FOINIX, gives us the number 700 = 500+70+10+50+10+60. The numerical value of words and letters is known as Gemetria. The well-known adage of 'the phoenix from the flames' is really referring to Kundalini activation as it travels to the third eye and sets it alight with its energy of fire.

According to the Ancient Chinese, a vital energy circulates through the body on the specific paths called 'meridians'. This vital energy makes surface on the skin with more than 700 different points. It is on the balancing of this vital energy of the body.

Tall stones have seven 'bands' of energy (range of energy). While the Earth Kundalini travels from the middle of the Earth up through the perineum, straight through the middle of the body, and out the top of the head, the body Kundalini begins at the base of the spine, travels up the spine, and out the top of the head. This requires preparation, balance, and purity of the body in order to facilitate such a transition. The seven bands equate to our chakras (energetic chakra bands) and our ancient ancestors utilised a powerful circular Earth energy pattern known as a 'primary halo'. It is highly magnetic and invariably consists of three concentric circles of energy, with standing stones and mounds sited upon them. This is the reason why the ancients chose a circular design for their stone circles, mounds, and sacred sites to mark their location within the esoteric landscape. 'Concentric' means of or denoting circles, arcs, or other shapes which share the same centre, the larger often completely surrounding the smaller. Blue stones were originally formed into an oval shape (the shape of our eyes which represent all-knowing). But, later, the Bluestones were arranged in a circle between the two rings of sarsens and in an oval at the centre of the inner ring. Constructing Europe's unusual Megalithic and Cyclopean architecture was based on a mysterious "technique" which involved tapping the strength of the "God within" by awakening the "Cyclopean", or third, eye. Preseli Bluestone (originally, outer circle) activates the Soma Chakra, located at the hairline above the third eye. This is a higher resonance of the third eye which, when activated, opens metaphysical awareness and visionary ability. It also has to do with perception of the cycles of time, awareness, and the workings of synchronicity. When this chakra is functioning well, it gives you the mental clarity necessary to achieve 'en-lighten-ment' and promotes lucid dreaming. It unites the pituitary gland that governs physical function with the pineal gland, transcendent spiritual awareness. Preseli Bluestone helps you connect to Earth energies and the wisdom of the Celtic Druidic peoples.

Bluestone assists you to move beyond time to access the past or future, and this is the reason it was chosen. A megalith should be regarded as a semiconductor 'macrochip' (large electronics - opposite of microchip), which has the capacity to store and transmit energy. They are energy beams that connect all stone circles across the landscape using Earth energy. Sited upon Earth energy geometries, they absorb and transmit energy (energy grids networks). They are geodetic-megalithic energy, of which there are several in any stone circle. They generate geodetic energies. The rising of Earth's Kundalini (Serpent) that happens within and through us connects with the 'Unity Consciousness Grid'. There are four aspects of self, physical, mental, emotional and spiritual that forms a circle of our being. A circle requires all of its points to be equi-distant from its centre. That centre point is you, the individual and all must be in balance.

To support our greatest well-being, and to make possible our evolution and spiritual awakening, we must allow ourselves (and our brainwave patterns) to breathe in concert with Mother Earth and with her natural cycles moment-to-moment. The Earth is a spherical receiver of cosmic energy (evolutionary intelligence) which directs our biological process and spiritual evolutionary unfoldment.

The Earth re-radiates the cosmic information it receives from its core outward in complex longwave signals. We receive these signals via our spinal columns and cranial structures (a vertical antenna system). The cranial cavity, the capstone to this antenna, captures this information and refocuses it to the pineal gland, a neuro-endocrine transducer in the centre of the brain, where it is then transmitted (via the hypothalamus) as signals that direct the pituitary gland, the master control centre of the brain. These signals are further distributed via the rest of the neurological system. In planetary harmonics, the frequency of Venus activates the pineal gland and has a consciousness raising frequency. Pi is also pinnacle. All afterlife realms exist as afterlife dimensions inhabiting the same space, just at different frequencies or vibrations. Tracking Venus also gave rise to the Megalithic Yard (MY), a distance of 2.72 metres also known as 'Euler's number' which is a fraction short of pi. Venus was important to the builders of Stonehenge and also in modern day society as it represents the pentagram, taking a pentagram-shaped orbit, and is therefore connected to the number 5, the fifth element, the ether, and not forgetting its hertz consciousness raising frequencies too, vibrating at 442 hertz. This is the real reason for Stonehenge; it was a cosmic power station to awaken the consciousness of the individuals who were present, taking them to greater places using the energy and power of Earth transmitted through themselves as an antennae.

So, there you have it, Stonehenge was an energy grid used to harness Earth's serpent Kundalini energy and, in turn, to transmute their own chakra system into cosmic consciousness, the God-Head or God-state.

MORE ABOUT STONEHENGE:

The altar stone is off-centre, as it was built upon a 'Yin Aquifer' that records sacred information of the sacred site. In alchemy, the water and the fire lead to the initiate being the dragon master. Fire and water incarnates the inner dragon of wisdom, the philosopher's stone.

When you overcome the dragon (slay the dragon, the alchemical dragon) you become the 'Sons of the Dragon' and you become the hierophant who is someone that understands the sacred mysteries and esoteric principles.

The Merlin stone, as it is also called, has significance, as Merlin is symbolic of the inner wizardry of self (inner alchemy – philosopher's stone). The Moon has an impact on water, therefore it was important to monitor its location by a lunar calendar.

The trilithon represents the three essences of alchemy.

They are 13 feet high and 7 feet wide, 13 = death, after which there is a resurrection and transformation (as with 12 disciples + Christ = 13) and 7 = end of cycle. It is the end of the old you in place of a new you.

There were originally 30 of them, and 30 means a connection to a higher force.

The Avenue and Heel stone is the end of individual consciousness and the entry into unity consciousness.

Each sacred site represents a planet or a planetary orbit called a planisphere. Silbury Hill represents Earth and Mars. Each planet represents a metal of alchemy. Saturn = Lead (Black)/Jupiter = Tin/Moon = Silver (White)/Mercury = Mercury/Mars = Iron (Red)/

Venus = Copper/Sun = Gold. This is why the summer solstice is so important as it represents enlightenment, the gold of alchemy.

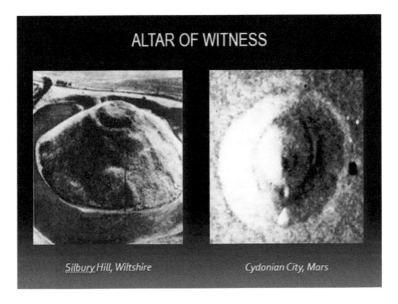

(Altar of Witness – Largest Mound in Europe)

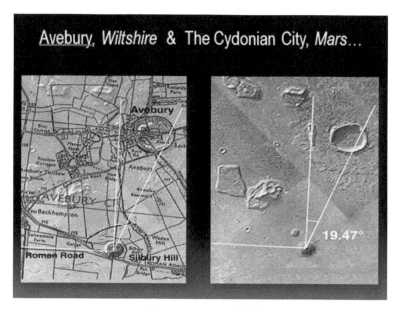

(Exact Map Overlay)

More Mars – Stonehenge connections:

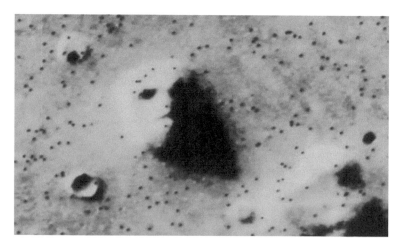

(The face on Mars)

The famous face on Mars has grid latitude of 4523.893421 which, when divided by 2160 (zodiac significance), it equals 97.3386882, which gives us both the diameter and location of Stonehenge in a clear planetary correlation.

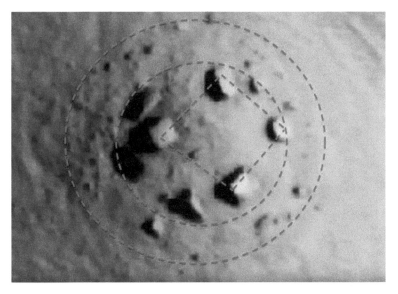

(Mars-Henge)

There is also another intriguing display of intergalactic mathematics ('mathematics' derives from 'Mathema', which means 'to know') which has been discovered by mathematician Carl Munck, acting as a pyramid matrix system and a universal satellite navigation system. This set of numerical sequences has a hidden code that reveals the location of other monuments of both Earth and Planet Mars encoded within the diameters of that particular monument. This is how it works. Stonehenge, in Wiltshire, is a 360 degree circle that has 60 outer stones and 15 centre blocks. When we use the mathematical formula 360x60, it equals 21,600, which is a multiple of 51degrees divided by 10 divided by 42.35 (51 degrees + 10 minutes 42.35 seconds); the exact location of Stonehenge. Stonehenge is 288 feet across which, when multiplied by 15 (centre block number) divided by the square root 15, we get 15.562, which is the exact grid longitude of Stonehenge. 52.562 divided by 360 pi equals a square root of 2160, which is the number of years each zodiac sign rules. Square root 2160 divided by 2 pi is the grid reference of the 3 smaller pyramids in Egypt, which are adjacent to the Great Pyramid and the two other larger pyramids, which equals the square root 2.71, the megalithic yard, and 2.72 which is known as Euler's number. 360 divided by the megalithic yard squared equals the radius of the Great Pyramid itself. When we use a 3-dimensional formation of the Great Pyramid using double pi, we get 9929.184896, which is the encoded grid latitude of the pyramid of the Cydonian city on Planet Mars. And, in addition to this, the famous face on Mars has a grid latitude of 4523.893421 which, when divided by the square root 2160, equals 97.3386882; the diameter of Stonehenge.

This correlation between encoded mathematical coordinates also extends to other pyramids and sacred monuments too, such as in Mexico and elsewhere around the globe. It demonstrates a secret code of numbers there to guide others to certain locations between the two planets of Earth and Mars represented by Silbury Hill.

Stonehenge itself represents Saturn, which is the God of Stones amongst many other things, even time (Chronos).

Modern man believes that he has the most updated knowledge of our existence and we are supposedly now at the pinnacle of human development in its most current year and time. We regard all that has gone before us, especially our ancient past occupied by our ancient ancestors, as being primitive and basic. Or, at least that is what we're told publically. We are told that the likes of the Pyramids of Egypt were built by Hebrew slaves who transported large and heavy stones for miles and erected them over 400 feet high in the desert using only the most basic of tools. We are told that ancient man had basic knowledge and used stones to create cosmic calendars to map out the year, which is partly true, as the planets influence us and our chakra system with each planet ruling a certain chakra, therefore it was important to know where a particular planet is/was in the sky to enhance that chakra balancing, hence star maps, but it goes much deeper. And their knowledge is far more advanced than we give them credit for; in fact, they had more knowledge of the workings of the human body, its energy systems, and its self than we do today.

They knew how to extract information from their own DNA, and they knew how to advance their own physical vessels. They understood Earth's meridians and used them to create their own God-state consciousness. They were more in tune with nature and knew how to connect to it to get their higher levels of themselves activated. They were much more connected to their world than we are today, and they were not disconnected by fancy electrical devices of the 21st century that actually takes us away from our true essence.

All cultures talk about the same subject, and they have left us a transcript within their famous monuments and mythical Gods and Goddesses. That message is about our true self, our true essence, and how to achieve the God-state, the higher mind! And despite popular belief that these cultures were a separate entity, they were not, they were deeply connected and had the same knowledge base, which means that they had communications of some kind between themselves or even with a higher aspect overseeing everything and co-ordinating from a greater panoramic viewpoint. This can be proven beyond any doubt by mathematics and other means. All the famous monuments of Earth, and even further afield on Planet Mars, are connected by mathematical co-ordinates that give the exact locations of each other that are contained within their diameters and proportions. This is impossible without co-ordination of the greatest heights. The universe is a mathematical design, and all things large and small on Earth, and in the cosmos, follow a mathematical code. Even the foetus grows to a mathematical grid. From the nautilus shell of the snail to the large plasma pinch effect of spiral galaxies, all are encoded. Maths is a universal language that we are only touching the surface of, even in our modern era. And a thought that I lay in bed pondering. If infinity is greater than any number and the universe is in-fact number then the creative force must be greater than the universe.

This is an ancient principle of enlightenment used by all the famous cultures that I have mentioned in this book. It is a linear channel of cosmic energy from the core of Earth through the human body and into the ether during our Kundalini awakening. This has been practised extensively throughout our ancient ancestral history and is still today by the initiates of certain organisations who have retained this in-depth knowledge purely for themselves. The general populous will never know this knowledge, as they are falsely taught about their reality which is created for them by the same groups of initiates and 'Brotherhoods'. The simple fact is we do not know about our self, we do not even consider our capabilities, and we are never accurately taught about these things. Until we understand ourselves, we can never reach our true potential and we can never access our rightful inheritance, namely knowledge. We must understand that we are multi-faceted and multi-dimensional, and we are the make-up of the stars, planets, and the cosmos.

A New Look At Crop Circles:

Even crop circles that are largely located around the region of Stonehenge contain hidden encrypted messages within sound called 'diatonic ratios'.

(Crop Formation)

Crop circles are a message through musical cryptology.

You arrive in Wiltshire and you await the rest of your small party of investigators, in this case, British actor, Danny Dyer, and his documentary film crew.

You say your hello and the introductions are underway.

You visit new and recent geospiral pictures on the landscape together and you feel the buzzing sensation of their energy as you venture within the geometric outlines.

When we see a snowflake and its beautiful patterns, we don't often realise that this is the shape of the sound of the environment around it and that the shape of that snowflake is purely a recreation of that sound's geometric patterns. It is mimicking the environmental sound.

Of course there are the fake crop circles that Doug and Dave claim to have created, although crop circles were recorded as early as the year 1590. But, on the whole, there is an advanced numerical mystique about them, which I will detail in a moment. I once asked someone on social media who was claiming to have created crop circles how he had encoded diatonic ratios within his design. He had no clue what I was talking about and could not answer my question. Therefore, he had not created them!

People have seen, and even filmed, plasma balls of light forming some crop circles, some have even identified an intelligent binary communication between the individual plasma balls as if they are working together with a consciousness. They also have striking resemblance to the Foo-Fighters of WWII that followed aircrafts through the skies.

When people film and see plasma balls of light above an area which then sees a crop circle appear, this is microwave energy and flash heat that causes one side of the crop to be elongated and therefore curved without damage. This curvature gives us the crop circle formation using microwave energy, which is a form of the universal energy electromagnetism. At this point, take your mind back to Chapter 1 and the section on vacuum domains. To reiterate:

Vacuum domains are self-radiant balls of light/ionised gas that occur when an electron separates from its parent atom, this can be guided by thought and can react to thought as the wavelengths are similar. They are luminous effects created by combined forces of electromagnetics and gravitational principles that can manifest localised mini black holes of gravispin, creating a vacuum effect and a pulsed heat release. They are a 'noosphere', from 'nous' meaning intellect/mind, a "Sphere Of Human Thought". These balls of light have been seen creating crop circles, and crop circles contain diatonic ratios which are an intelligent communication through sound; it may even be a message hidden within soundwaves. The balls of light that have been recorded creating crop circles have also been recorded as having intelligent communication between one another.

Therefore, if vacuum domains are created by thought and the mind, then whose mind is creating crop circles?

If electrons are floating around freely, even for a very short amount of time, they can be shoved far away from their point of origin by the electric field and then shoved back. And then forwards again. As they move back and forth, they crash into air molecules in the air that can knock electrons in them to higher-energy orbits. Then, these electrons fall back, emitting light.

But, there is more. For those who have seen the 1980's movie 'Close Encounters of the Third Kind', you will know that, at the end of the film, there is a communication between humans and extra-terrestrials by use of music. And the Greeks called Geometry 'frozen music', which leads me onto my next point.

Some of the great composers, such as Mozart and Bach, used to deliberately hide cryptic messages within their compositions, to be deciphered by the chosen recipient. Bach used to spell his name with musical notes that formed part of his compositions.

It is called musical cryptology.

It is the transmission of a message through music. Musical notes

A – G are used to spell out words, abbreviations, and codes.

They can transport secret messages through music and are the perfect camouflage. Musical notes are also geometric shapes.

Music can also lead to encounters with realities beyond everyday consciousness and open inner doors to other dimensions.

Within crop circles (the majority of them), diatonic ratios have been found hidden within the crop circles themselves. Diatonic ratios are basically the white keys of a piano, and are a human response to sound. This being the case, it would the perfect way to encode a message for humans. Diatonic ratios are simple whole numbers that determine a scale of musical notes, and the only place in nature that diatonic ratios are found is in bird calls and whales. These ratios have been found to have their own intelligence.

What if musical cryptology, in the form of a crop circle, is a hidden message for humanity? What if there is a clandestine communication going on beneath our noses? Not just by a pictorial shape, but by sound.

And what if, with each new crop circle that appears, we are being given a new note that continues from the last note to eventually complete a musical sentence that gives us the full and complete message through harmonics and sonics? The higher the frequency and pitch, the more complex the shape of a crop circle is.

I think it is a cryptic message hidden within Geometry. The law of Geometry governs mathematical intervals of notes, and diatonic ratios have been found hidden within crop circles.

The answer to the message of the crop circle is in the scale of human sound responses. The messages of the crop circles even go into the fifth postulate of interpretation of non-Euclidean Geometry, which is a theorem.

The monuments of the world contain hidden coded messages and act as radio wave transmitters and receivers to other places.

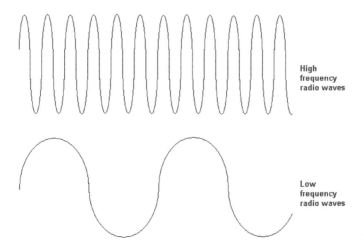

(Two radio waves together can be used to carry hidden messages)

And wherever in the world they are located, or whatever shape they are formed, the story is the same.

They are the first computers on Earth - they are gigantic motherboards and resonance chambers.

We live in a world of hidden codes and, once we decipher them, our world changes.

SIX

ATLANTIS AND LEMURIA: IT'S ALL IN THE HEAD

'Atlantis' means 'Island of Atlas', and it was first spoken and written about by Plato.

In Sanskrit, 'Atl' means 'to support or uphold', as Atlas was said to hold the world on his shoulders. In the Nahuatl language, we find immediately the radical 'a', 'atl', which signifies water, war, and the top of the head. Why the top of the head? The word 'atl' is found in the names of most of their Gods, and one of its meanings is 'top of the head'.

It is the idea of one island ruling over seven, which refers to the chakra system of the body, as I will explain in a moment.

The tree sacred to Atlas, its branches, like his arms, supported the heavens. The oak's association with Atlas implies a primeval tree cult or pillar cult, a memory of it surviving in Kritias, Plato's Atlantis account, when he described a ceremonial column at the very midpoint of the Temple of Poseidon, itself located at the centre of Atlantis. The tree also has Druid connotations, as the word 'Druid' means 'oak knowledge'.

The pineal gland (6th chakra, the third-eye) lies at the geometrical centre point of the brain. Plato's account of Atlantis described a *"ceremonial column at the very midpoint of the Temple of Poseidon, itself located at the centre of Atlantis"*. The ceremonial column (Oak Tree, Tree of Life, Staff of Moses, etc.) is the human spine with 33 vertebrae.

The actual medical term for the 33rd vertebrae which holds up the skull is 'Atlas', same as the King of Atlantis. In Atlantean mythology, Atlas holds up the world, or the Heavens, and, in your body, the Atlas vertebrae holds up your head/mind. In Atlantean mythology, Atlas has 7 daughters who spend all their time guarding and dancing around the Tree of Life, and in your body, you have 7 energy centres (chakras) dancing around your spine, with the spine being the Tree of Life.

Plato described Atlantis as being shaped like three concentric circles of land separated by concentric circles of water, in other words, the shape of a bullseye. Why would the centre of a target be called a 'bullseye'?

The Atlas vertebra holds up your brain, your 'third-eye' is at the centre of your brain, and the centre of Atlantis is a 'bullseye'. In fact, your skull, which Atlas holds up, is shaped just like Atlantis is described. At the centre point is your third-eye. The third-eye is separated and surrounded completely by water/fluid. Your third-eye comes into contact with your cerebrospinal fluid at its third ventricle.

And, lastly, around that is the skull. Plato said sacrificial bull's blood was shed over the exterior of the Temple of Poseidon, which is also consistent with the blood that flows over the exterior of the brain.

"Bulls were associated with divine regents in Sumer, Egypt, Assyria, Minoan Crete, Greece, Rome, Iberia, and Ireland. All of these cultures featured traditions of a great deluge from which their ancestors came with all the accoutrements of a high civilisation, including, most importantly, matters of kingship. In each people, their king was ritually identified with a sacred bull, because it was important for a leader to identify with the tremendous strength and aggressiveness epitomised by such an animal."

In pre-Celtic Ireland, the new monarch had to undergo a ceremonial bath of bull's broth, which he then drank from an Atlantean-like golden cup.

If the Temple of Poseidon (between your 'temples') is your brain, then Atlantis' bullseye is your third-eye/pineal gland, which literally "roams free in the courtyard of the temple" because it is surrounded by cerebrospinal fluid.

So there you have it; Atlantis is the third-eye of the human brain that enables spiritual sight and spiritual consciousness. So, what about the much spoken about, within the New Age, Atlantean and Lemurian crystals and their re-activation?

I have already mentioned that Lemuria is the pituitary gland and that MU is code for the light of Sirius which is a 33rd degree initiation frequency, the blazing star of freemasonry. It is also why one of the shafts of the Great Pyramid faces towards, and connects to, this planet. Between the pineal gland and the pituitary gland, there is a region in the brain called 'the crystal palace', and this is the meaning of the re-activation of the Atlantean and Lemurian crystals. Again, it refers to human consciousness. The crystal skull story is also indicating divine consciousness and consciousness beyond the body. It is the risen messiah, the supernal light transmission (Supernal = sky). It is the communication of the light presence and the light power and light transmission.

So, together in Atlantis and Lemuria, we have the masculine and feminine aspects of inner brain consciousness combined, a mystical marriage and a mystical union.

Many ancient symbols, albeit they have different connotations today, were originally symbols of consciousness and a perfect example of this is Baphomet. Today, Baphomet is associated with Satan (which I will cover later).

(Baphomet)

Esoterically, Baphomet is a symbol of initiation into the secret mysteries. It is a phrase for Father of the Temple and is stated as *'Temple Omnium Hominum Pads Abba'* which gives us TEM OHP AB, spelling Baphomet backwards. The He-goat is symbolic of as above, so below, the elemental energies of the Heavens above and the fallen energies of Earth below.

The father is the Hippocampus and the temple is the head. 'Hippo' means 'horse' and 'campus' (Kampos) means 'sea monster' or 'sea horse'. This is why we see depictions of Poseidon riding seahorses. *"In my father's house there are many rooms,"* in other words, the mind (house/temple) has many compartments!

(Symbol of Father of the Temple)

Poseidon is the God of the sea and water, and includes being the ruler of the pineal gland which is surrounded by water, namely the cerebrospinal fluid. The horns of the hippocampus are 'Ammons Horn' and Amon/Amun means hidden, even Moses is sometimes shown with such horns. The hippocampus relates to learning and it is an ancient Gnosis and science known as the oracle or the holy of holies. The trident of Poseidon is shin (fire), the three prongs known as the trishula, three spears.

Poseidon and the temple can then lead us onto the myth of the Lost City of Atlantis which is, again, code for our own consciousness.

SEVEN

IN THE BEGINNING WAS THE WORD

Over the forthcoming chapters, I am going to take you through a journey of self-discovery in a way known only previously by those chosen to know the secrets of creation, the initiates and priesthoods. Before I move onto the word, I will share a few other little bits of esoteric knowledge with you. And I will use the most read and most famous book the world has ever seen.

Matt 13:10-11 states that *"the knowledge of the secrets of the kingdom of heaven has been given to you, but not to them"* (them being the uninitiated)

Mark 4: 10-11 states *"the secret of the kingdom of God has been given to you, but to those on the outside everything is said in parables"*

A parable is a defined as such:

A simple story used to illustrate a moral or spiritual lesson.

People have believed the story and have missed the spiritual lesson. They have missed the double meanings of the scriptures, which are merely now a script. Just ask yourself why Jesus is known as the greatest story ever told, because it's a story, and that story hides a deeper truth, and that truth has been missed. The physical Jesus is a fiction.

Man and woman are, in fact, a microcosm of the macrocosm and we are the universe in miniature.

What happens above happens below in a synergy, a medical-astrology. The way in which the planets of the solar system orbit the Sun is mimicked by electrons orbiting the nucleus of DNA, and so on. That being the case, we are all Gods and we are all an aspect of all else. Biblical characters and stories are metaphors that hide this truth, and hide the truth of our own greatness from us by directing the focus without instead of where it should be, within.

The kingdom of God is within you – Luke 17:21

We have a choice, however. The head of John the Baptist was taken to Damascus (I will talk about John the Baptist later). But what is Damascus? It is our choice. The road to Damascus is a term that signifies a great change, where Saul/Paul was converted. In Arabic, Damascus is called Ash-Shām, which means *'Land On The Left Hand'* or *'Land Of The Right Hand'*, depending on the region. The Right Hand Path and Left Hand Path are two opposing philosophies. The Right Hand Path is the submission to a higher power and the Left Hand Path downplays the higher power. This is also white and black magic.

(Right-Hand Path Of The Heart Symbol)

We must repent, which relates to the number 5, and redirect inwards to the throne of his glory. The throne of his glory is our *Inner Re-Generative State*, enlightenment through the seat (throne) of our soul, the pineal gland. The number five is the pentagram and the ascension beyond the four, which represents the material and physical realms. It is an important esoteric number and, even within one of the most famous religious songs around the world, 'Hallelujah', the final chord has five notes comprised of five different frequencies that have wave fronts that, when super-imposed, form a five-pointed geometric star. The pentagram within the pentacle is also important in Islam. The points of the pentagram touch the circle of the pentacle every 72 degrees, and Venus in zodiac astrological terms is the sub-ruler of Virgo which, in Latin, means virgin. Venus is symbolised as the pentagram, as it has a pentagram-shaped orbit. Add these component parts together and we get the 72 virgins, a fake promise. Venus has an influence in the Islamic religion in terms of astro-theology, as does the Moon.

So, do we become Samson, which means Sun (light/conscious), or do we become Delilah, which means the door to darkness and betray our Samson, our own light? (D – 'daleth' means 'door' and 'Lilah' means 'darkness'). Do we become Abel and have the ability to think before we act, or do we become Cain and act without thinking, demonstrating our animalistic nature? And we can see in the actions of many people their animalistic nature clothed in human form, animal souls in human form; animals have territories and so do humans but we call them countries, which are just larger territories. Do we choose Jesus Barabbas or do we choose our Jesus Christ? In other words, our own inner ego or our own inner divinity? The choice is ours and we must overcome our Didymus, the real name of Thomas as in 'doubting Thomas', meaning duality or two minds. Our mind must become unified as one. Are we Icarus who was told not to fly too close to the sea, which means a low attachment to earthly things and he was told not to fly too high or close to the Sun, which is telling us of a fascination with fire. That restless desire of knowing, the intellectual presumption and clmbing for knowledge. Intellectul arrogance punished by the infernal fall (underworld) leading to divine ignorance. Faith is the cause of ignorance. He who has knowledge (gnosis) of the truth is free and those with ignorance (agnoia) is a slave. The lating aside of ignorance through slef-knowledge guarantees salvation which is always self-redemption not redemption by another. Man is perfectable through knowledge. The heretic necessity of knowing or restlessly investigating the truth. Knowledge has the power to spur man beyond his animal condition. Faith is to be divided and not fully intergrated lacking epignosis, which is self-recognition of our godly nature or true reality. Don't have faith, have knowledge!

I have devised a blueprint that spans the whole ancient world, through the Egyptians, Sumerians, and the Annunaki, South Americans, Mayans, Babylonians, Moai of Easter Island, Atlantis and Lemuria, Stonehenge and other monolithic sites, Nazca Lines, crop circles, that even connect to monuments on Planet Mars, etc., and right the way through all religious scriptures. Even into myths and legend, such as King Arthur. From that blueprint, I can say that the message left for us is the same, as the ancients had access to the same self-knowledge base. That message is of the creation of a higher type of human and one of enlightened consciousness.

I will reference some of these ancient cultures as we go along but I will concentrate largely on Christianity, as stated, and, of course, I will take you into Ancient Egypt and touch upon her secrets because it has a bearing on Christianity. But, whichever ancient culture I could have highlighted, it all leads to the same place – YOU, and how YOU can reconnect to your greater origin.

THE REAL BOOK OF REVELATION:

'Revelation' means 'to reveal', and that is what I am going to do. Revelation is the book of messianic Kabbalah, in other words, to receive the Christ knowledge, and it tells us about recapturing the lost knowledge and wisdom of the Bible. It is the power of inner transformation. The messianic Kabballah is the power and wisdom to develop and maintain the purity of one's thoughts, feelings, emotions, and desires in life.

Without this, there are all kinds of impurities, evil thoughts, lustfulness, selfishness, destruction, and animalistic will. Churches have become impure and their direction of worship is now apostasy (disaffiliation/abandonment). But, because of leaven (carnality), the churches have lost the messianic Kabbalah and they have become spiritually dead.

In Revelation 1:17, it states, *"When I saw him I fell at his feet as dead"*, which really means the death of ego at the feet of our Christified being. The 7 Churches of revelation are the 7 energy/magnetic centres of the body, namely the 7 chakras which we need to cleanse and purify to allow our ascending serpent, Kundalini, to pass through unblocked. A horse is symbolic of our driving force and, within Revelation, we have the famous four horsemen of the Apocalypse. They, too, have esoteric meaning. The red horse is the fiery solar light in the Christified body, the Krestos (Fire), and the white horse is the physical body/Christic lightening. The pale horse is the mental body and the black horse is kama rupa, or the body of desires. We can see similar metaphors in the centaur, which is 'Ken-taur' or 'Khan-taur' meaning 'torch/light' and 'Taur' derives from 'Taurus', the bull which shows us power and control over our animalistic nature. That is why the man is the top half of the bull on the centaur. That, in a nutshell, is the meaning of the book of Revelation.

Russian scientists are now saying that DNA follows the same rules as all of our human languages. To this end, they compared the rules of syntax (the way in which words are put together to form phrases and sentences), semantics (the study of meaning in language forms), and the basic rules of grammar. They found that the alkaline of our DNA follows a regular grammar and do have set rules just like our languages. So human languages did not appear coincidentally, but are a reflection of our inherent DNA. Scientists believe that the human DNA is arranged in such a precise way that it reveals a set of arithmetic patterns and ideographic symbolic language. This is the basis of Egyptian hieroglyphs and even the Nazca Line land patterns, as both are a pictogram language, also known as an ideogram or ideograph. Human beings are a three billion letter code, and this figure doesn't include the dormant DNA (what science wrongly calls 'junk DNA') which is yet to be activated. Time can, of course, be manipulated by such things as time dilation and, as you approach a black hole of space, time slows down as black holes emit a frequency of 460 hertz, which slows down time and can change brainwave states. Within our DNA, we also have black holes called vacuum domains. The black holes of the brain are connected to the black holes of space (planetophysical physics). 460 hertz are isochronic tones, which are brainwave entrainment, and they are an audio-based way to stimulate your brainwave activity.

They can guide your dominant brainwave activity to a different frequency, changing your mental state into a meditative state. In DNA, vacuum domains can cause patterns in the vacuum-producing magnetised wormholes, which are microscopic equivalents of universal wormholes. There are tunnel connections between entirely different areas in the universe, through which information can be transmitted outside of space and time. The DNA attracts these bits of information and passes them onto our consciousness, and this is a form of hyper-communication. Wise ones would download sacred knowledge through their crown chakra in this way.

Vacuum domains are self-radiant balls of light/ionised gas that occur when an electron separates from its parent atom. This can be guided by thought and can react to thought as the wavelengths are similar. They are luminous effects created by combined forces of electromagnetics and gravitational principles that can manifest localised mini black holes of gravispin, creating a vacuum effect and a pulsed heat release. These balls of light have been seen creating crop circles, and crop circles contain diatonic ratios which are an intelligent communication through sound; it may even be a message hidden within soundwaves. The balls of light that have been recorded creating crop circles have also been recorded as having intelligence communication between one another.

(Group-focused consciousness can create vacuum domains)

Zulus call crop circles 'Izishoze Zamatongo' which means 'writings of the Gods', and they were first recorded in Europe in 1590, although in some parts of the world earlier than that.

So, what is the relevance of this? Well it leads us onto the word, where everything was spoken into existence. If language is a reflection of our inherent DNA, then that too was spoken into existence through the power of manifestation. We, as Gods, must also then have that capability, and this is called the 'law of attraction', a universal creative power detailed in the book of St Thomas, which was removed from the Bible by agents of the Church. Why, does someone not want us to have this knowledge?

The word, therefore, is creation spoken into existence, a manifestation of a thought or an idea.

I mentioned nostrils and breath within the chapter on Egypt during the section about the Sphinx, and this is also relevant now. This is because we are told that God breathed into the nostrils of Adam. In Hebrew, Adam is 'aleph-daleth-mem' (ADM), and Eve is 'Hei-Vav-Hei'. 'Aleph' means 'the God-man' which is connected by the body (Eden), Upper Heaven to Lower Earth. The connection between man and God is the womb. When we look at the Hebrew word for Eden, we get Nun-Dal-Ghah. 'Dal' is 'daleth', which means 'doorway', therefore the doorway to Eden is the yoni. 'Nun' means creational waters, again, referring to the yoni/womb.

When we look at the word 'Iod-Hei-Vav-Hei', we get a word that is 'God' in Hebrew, and this is how.

Iod = 10, Iod-Hei = 15, Iod-Hei-Vav = 21, and Iod-Hei-Vav-Hei = 26. Together this is 72, the number of God in Hebrew. 'Iod-Hei-Vav-Hei' is 'Phallus-Uterus-Man-Woman'. Therefore, Adam and Eve were made in the image of God, as we find both Adam (Vav) and

Eve (Hei) within God; Iod-Hei-Vav-Hei (72).

(Left Arm of the Pentagram is Adam and Right Arm is God, 'Iod-Hei-Vav-Hei' – 'from God came Adam' – microcosm from the macrocosm, from the pentagram (five/ether) to the tetragram - four/material realm. The pentagram is also known as the microcosmic star)

In this case, Adam, or man, is Vav, which is the sixth letter of the Hebrew alphabet and therefore corresponds to the number 6. Adam was created on the sixth day and this is because of that connection to the number six. Hei is the fifth letter of the Hebrew alphabet and therefore corresponds to the number 5. Together, this is 11, and I have mentioned 5 and 6 and 11 previously when squaring the circle through the marriage of Isis and Osiris 6/5. ADM = 9, which is the number of completion. In the Hebrew Tree of Life, the Sephirot, Hei is within man, which gives us Eve from Adam. Hei also represents creation.

The Bible tells us that Adam came first followed by Eve. Nature, however, tells us that woman came first before man and therefore if woman is the doorway to Eden, which she is, then woman must surely have come first, confirming nature's evidence.

Just something to ponder: if Adam and Eve had three sons, then how did they populate the Earth? And if they did have daughters that are not mentioned in the Bible, then we are all a result of incest! The only other biblical way would have been copulation with their mother, Eve, which is also incest.

Now, for more on the Adam and Eve story. Adam and Eve is the event of androgyny separated into duality, and the rib of Adam is symbolic of two halves of a whole. Our inner wisdom can be expressed through speech (word of God), but if we misuse the fifth chakra (throat chakra) which contains Adam's apple, this lack of wisdom can result in the fall of man in Eden (body). After all, we spell words as they can cast spells and be used for bad, not good. The first pen was the tongue.

The vocal cord resembles the female yoni, the Sanskrit word for 'vagina', and this is where the word is gestated. The throat and the yoni are the two mouths united. When you sing a hymn, it is a word that derives from the word 'hymen'. In Egypt, this throat and yoni connection is the Egyptian Goddess of motherhood, Isis. The first IS = the throat, and the second IS = the genitalia that, when purified, incarnates the solar force, RA, or Christ, through a virgin birth of inner chastity.

(The two mouths at the Royal courts of justice in London)

This is also the case with the Hei-Hei of the Hebrew Iod-Hei-Vav-Hei. In the Sephirot, the Hebrew Tree of Life, death is the doorway to knowledge as the throat connects the body to the head, representing the element of sound (the word/speech).

In order to knock on this doorway to knowledge, you need to know where to look. There are two potential outcomes of using this door, which are good and evil. In the Kaballah, the throat is daath/knowledge, which is traditionally never spoken or revealed. It is the great arcanum, secret knowledge hidden from humanity. The famous logo for the apple company, with a bite mark, is symbolic of the misuse of speech.

The 9th Commandment of God – *Thou shall not bear false witness* – is referring to truthful and effective speech. So, why the apple? When you slice an apple width ways, you get the geometric shape

173

of the pentagram. Not only is the pentagram representative of the fifth element, the ether, God, but it is also the number five (5) and so is Eve (Hei) number five, giving us the apple and Eve connection.

(Apple sliced width ways = the pentagram)

The serpent on the tree is referring to wisdom and enlightenment, and I will deal with this more in the Christ section later. So, there you are, Adam and Eve are male and female energy from God, whose existence was separated from androgyny into duality incarnated into Eden, the human body. The four rivers of Eden, the Hiddekel, Euphrates, Pishon, and Gihon, where Eden is said to be located, are the sexual energy of the masculine and feminine combined. The Ida and Pingala also run each side of the body, and these are the biblical two witnesses of revelation and also the two olive trees.

It is stated in some versions that Adam's first wife was really Lilith. Lilith is, however, the dark side of Malkuth (physical world/body) and means 'of the darkness'. Lilith is desire and temptation, and the first sphere of the Hebrew Sephirot where the initiate enters the Tree of Life. The vile and traumatic experience called circumcision; we are told that circumcision is for hygiene and medical reasons, but it isn't!

So what is its origin?

The origin is in the Hebrew Scriptures regarding a character called Lilith who had a fall out with Adam and fled from Eden; she was the proto-type of Eve (this is their version, not mine). She was allowed to remain isolated, a witch, the mother of all demons, and to kill infants up until their naming day, 7 days for girls and 8 days for boys. The circumcision of boys occurs on the 8th day after birth, which is no coincidence!

The act and practice of circumcision is really a ritual to appease Lilith and her blood thirsty desire to do harm.

Adam and Eve is all of us, they are a metaphor, it is the splitting of primeval man into two and, as Plato explained, *"the primeval man was round, his back and sides forming a circle, and he had four hands and four feet, one head".* This is the real meaning of a twin flame, the two aspects of self. It is the polar opposite of our self, our duality that creates our inner union, self-balance. We are one separated into two. Duality makes us a twin, 50/50. Your own masculine and your own feminine are two halves of self, you are a twin. In Gnosticism. love is the union of opposites – love thyself. Love is turning yourself into a vessel of fulfilment for the other person. This only exists in the spirit world. In physicality we are really referring to attraction brought by hormones and fulfilling self. Both partners knowing the reason for their existence is a spiritual connection, which is love.

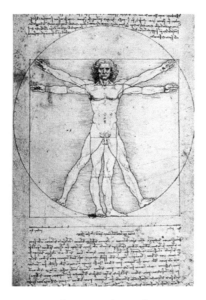

(Primeval Man)

And There Were Giants In Those Days:

There were giants on the earth in those days, and also after that, when the Sons of God came in unto the daughters of men – Genesis 6:4.

So what does this biblical passage really mean, does it mean that there was once a race of giants living upon the Earth, or is there a deeper hidden meaning to it?

It is apparent when you look at species many millions of years ago and you look at species of today that they appear to resemble each other, only a much smaller version. On that basis, you cannot rule out that giants did exist. But there is also a metaphorical meaning to them.

These giants were known as the Nephilim, and the word 'Nephilim' derives from a root word 'Naphal' which means 'to fall short', another meaning of sin. This brings us straight back to my blueprint that the ancients were really telling us about enlightenment and human consciousness through sexual forces and by other means. The Nephilim were also called the Watchers, meaning 'awake' or 'he who is awake', which is a reference to consciousness. We also get the word 'bishop' through the etymology of the word 'watcher'. A bishop sits in a Cathedral which means seat, which is the seat of illumination, the pineal gland.

A giant is a metaphor for a greater than average insight. It is symbolic of our greater and higher self and potential, and this is what this biblical passage and other references to giants really means. Even the Greeks and the Gods of Olympus have the same metaphorical meaning.

So, what about the Sons of God and the Daughters of Men?

In Masonry, which is a Jewish establishment (which I mention as the Bible is really the division of the Hebrew Scriptures and therefore relevant), this phrase is really referring to the 'Spiral Dance', which is a DNA upgrade from a double helix to a triple helix genetic. It is ascension through a genetic DNA upgrade.

It is referring to the procreation of the male (Square) and the earthly female (Masonic Compass logo).

Consciousness gives us a Godlike sense of the cosmos.

Whether we are discussing Jesus, Mary Magdalene, Mary and Joseph, Noah, Moses, Jonah and the Whale, Cain and Abel, etc., or the Pyramids of Egypt, Stonehenge, Atlantis, Easter Island, Nazca Lines, and many others, we are really discussing human consciousness and procreation, as my blueprint has discovered.

There were giants in those days. In other words, there were those of a higher knowledge and a higher insight, which is what the giant is symbolic of, a higher knowledge of self and the universe, who understood genetics (The Book of Genesis = The Book of Genetics/ Book of Genes) and how to raise their own frequency in order to achieve the philosopher's stone, enlightened consciousness. It also represents those who have the knowledge of sacred fertility. For example 'mushroom' (symbolic of the penis) is 'antimimon' in Greek, which has a Sumerian meaning of 'heavenly shade'. The root word of this in Greek is 'Gig-an-ti', which is 'gig-antes', which gives us the English word 'giant'.

(Cardinal Mushroom Attire & Mushroom at Saint Michael's Church, Hildesheim, Germany)

The magic mushroom, the Amanita Muscaria, opens your mind and takes you on a psychedelic journey of connection to other worlds, a fact known and a ritual practised by ancient priests and alike.

This information is retained by the chosen initiates of past and present.

EIGHT

CHRIST:
NOT A MAN BUT A METAPHOR

Who is this mystical man, Jesus, who walked Nazareth and cured the sick? Who is this man who, thousands of years later, is still worshipped the world over by people who dedicate their lives and existence to, and sometimes cannot make a decision, without calling upon him? The next two chapters are probably going to rock a few trees and generate scorn and hatred by those infatuated by a saviour because, quite frankly, they cannot deal with taking responsibility for themselves or their own lives.

They find it much easier to pass the responsibility to others and then ask for forgiveness. So, I will get right to the point: Jesus Christ was not a man, he never existed in the way people have been taught, and he is not coming back to save anyone. I am now about to disclose just who and what he is, and I make no apologies for doing so. If the human race is to advance, it needs to drop its childish behaviour and its stubborn belief systems that have resulted in murder and persecution, because these things do not belong in a higher mind or a higher state of being, and we are thousands of years behind where we should be because of controlling hypocritical belief systems. The human race is blind in a world where they could have x-ray vision. The Jesus story is set in the Age of Aquarius, which is the age of deception, but it is also the new initiate who receives the truth.

I have mentioned a number of times throughout this book of alchemical ascension through sexual alchemy and knowledge of the sexual union. The Jesus story continues with that theme. That is because this is what the story of Jesus is really telling us, and it is the real identity of Christ. You are now about to see how.

So it begins, an angel appears before Mary and tells her that she is to give birth to the son of God. Mary and Joseph trekked on a donkey to find a suitable location to deliver Christ to the world. The donkey, of course, is symbolic of the nephesh, which is the vital or bestial soul, and the child is the path of awakening, giving birth to the concept of the self being God. The birth in the manger is the first Venustic initiation (middle path) that we carry within ourselves, our inner Christ. This is the virgin birth of divine consciousness. Jesus was the son of Joseph which, in the Kabbalah, hides IO, which means the balance of the divine father and mother. It is the union that creates the Christ. Joseph is the Yesod, which corresponds to sexual energy and the sexual organs. In Latin, Maria is 'Ram-IO', which we have to read as "Mar" and backwards as "Ram". Ra is the fire and the letter 'M' (Mem) symbolises the water and the two polarities that release the dragon (serpent – wisdom). Fire and water are the masculine and feminine polarities in Malkuth. Mary is the material, the matter, the mater, and 'mater' means 'mother', which is the physical body. The black Madonna/black Mary symbolises the fire of enlightenment hidden within us, and the black Sun sometimes seen in churches is the first stage of Magnum Opus, the Great Work of alchemy.

(The Black Sun)

Upon their arrival, three wise men hear of the news and follow the Star of Bethlehem to locate the saviour. This Star of Bethlehem is the microcosmic star, the pentagram, which is the symbol of many mysteries. The pentagram leads wise men, those men who are wise, to their own inner divine realisation and their own inner Christ. Herod could not see or find the Star of Bethlehem as he lacked the wisdom to see the mysteries. Herod is symbolic of humanity as a whole. They brought with them frankincense, myrrh, and gold, which are conscious-raising components and gold, of course, is the philosopher's stone. Frankincense is transformation oil, as is Myrrh, which expands consciousness and raises awareness. Gold is wisdom.

The symbol of Christ giving us the holy trinity symbol with his hand and fingers is also the pentagram, however, the 'V for victory' sign given by the likes of war-time Prime Minister, Winston Churchill, is the inverted pentagram, which is the symbol of Satan. The story of Christ is not new, in fact, it was used many times before we even reached Jesus, Isis and Horus, Semiramis and Tammuz, and so on. The famous image of Christ, as accepted, is believed to be the son of Pope Alexander VI, namely Cesare Borgia.

(Cesare Borgia)

The story of Jesus is the story of the sacred sexual force, so is Satan, and so is Lucifer who is not the same character as Satan, despite widely-held belief. It tells us about sexual alchemy and the perfection of our sexual forces, which are the sexual priesthoods. We must rejoice, which means to have possession of or have the fruition of. Fruition is producing fruit and our fruit is our seed, sperm. Holding the orgasm thrusts sexual energy upwards, whereby we do not release the seed. This is the alchemical fire of transmutation, igniting each chakra until it reaches the pineal and pituitary glands, creating a spark of light that emits a halo, and the halo depicts the illuminated and enlightened mind. Jesus is the water of life which is semen, the 'sea of men'. This is where we can control the fish of the sea, the seed within the waters of life, sperm.

'Nazareth' derives from the verb 'Zara', which means 'to scatter/sow' or 'that which is sown', which is the seed/sperm. Incidentally, Nazareth didn't actually exist until the 2nd Century, so Jesus could not have been Jesus of Nazareth.

The cross is the insertion of the vertical phallus into the formal cteis, which forms a cross and is symbolising the sexual alchemy of transformation. It is the cross of initiation that we must place upon our shoulders. To take up the cross, as did Simon who carried the cross for Christ, is the work of holy alchemy. On the alchemical crucible, which is a container to smelt metal, it is the crux/cross where the initiate must suffer in order to destroy the animal soul through sexual transmutation. Simon comes from the Hebrew word 'shimon' which means to listen and, by listening, is how the pineal gland receives.

Between the sixth hour (Temptation) and the ninth hour (Sexual Magic), the initiate enters into the crucifixion of his spiritual night.

This is when we are told that Christ was crucified on the cross, which is purely symbolic. This is where the ego dies and the phoenix is reborn, the phoenix from the flames is enlightenment. The three nails of Christ (Krestos = esoterically means fire) that were used to fix Jesus to the cross symbolise the three purifications of iron and fire, which is the separation of the impure from the pure. There is, of course, another cross indicated by the hand gesture of the priests when giving the symbol of the cross on their body. It is the inverted cross of St Peter, which is the ninth sphere. In the first 3 gospels, the term 'king of the Jews' is repeated 12 times. This gives us 3x12=36. There were 36 knocks of the hammer that nailed Jesus to the cross. Joseph was 36 when he took Mary as his wife.

This inverted cross of St Peter, the ninth sphere, is what we need to escape by the correct use of sexual energy. The name Peter derives from 'Petrus', which means 'rock', and a rock is hard or 'to make hard', which is reference to an erection. The phrase *'get your rocks off'* means to ejaculate. The strange circle at the Vatican, the Sfera Con Sfera meaning 'sphere within a sphere' within the grounds of the Cortile (enclosed) Della (noble) Pigna (pinecone, pineal), is also symbolic of the ninth sphere.

(Sfera-con-sfera)

At the Vatican, when we look at St Peter's Square, we can see an obelisk inside the Vesica Piscis. The Vesica Piscis is formed by invisible geometry and is symbolic of the sexual act. It is not widely known that this stands upon an old Goddess temple and therefore we have the energy of opposites, enforced by the cross that it also stands upon, indicating the union of opposites too.

(St Peter's Square Obelisk – Obelisk means 'Baal's (Lord's) shaft')

The Hathors of Ancient Egypt believed that sexual energy was birthed in the solar plexus, which is known as Bethlehem, becoming the primal power for the ascent of consciousness. In Gnosticism, a virgin means to transform sexual energy through scientific chastity (abstention). A virgin is to know how to use the sexual force, whereby our matter then becomes pregnant with fire (Kundalini) and this is our inner virgin.

So why was Jesus a carpenter?

In the Aramaic (Semitic) language, the word for 'carpenter' is 'Nanger', which means 'serpent of wisdom'. In Hebrew, the Jewish messiah is known as 'the holy serpent'. 'Messiah' derives from the Hebrew 'Mashiah' meaning 'the anointed', which I will deal with soon. This sexual serpent energy can be used for compassion (Christ) or passion (Satan). The serpent Kundalini energy becomes a negative polarity if misused, becoming the descending serpent and the adversary meaning opposite, of the Christ force, which is the ascending serpent. When this fall occurs, the serpent Kundalini falls from the higher chakras, Heaven, and descends to the lower chakras, Earth. This is the fall of Satan from the Heavens. Early Christians called this force 'the devil'. Lucifer is our sexual force and, although similar to Satan, they are not one of the same. Lucifer is the Lux-Ferum (ferry), the carrier of light.

Satan, or in planetary terms Saturn, is Satanic consciousness, which is our lower sexual nature and sexual lust. This is why the world of pop music and alike is lustful, tainting the minds of the young with sex; it is Satanic consciousness and it rules the world.

The gates of Hell are male gonad glands that open and close to release semen, and Hell is the root chakra, which is red and known as the underworld that burns with the fire of Kundalini. Hell does not exist, it is a control mechanism. We must rise to escape this lower place which, in Islam, is known as salvation from hellfire.

When we use this sexual force for lustful passion, we are horny, which is reference to the horns of the devil. In Hebrew, Satan is written in three letters. שׂטן 'Shin' which is 'fire', 'Teth' which is 'serpent', and 'Yesod' which is our sexual force. In other words, the serpent fire of sexuality, at the base of the spine, Kundalini. Shin is also given to us by the hand symbol of Mr Spock in Star Trek and his race, Vulcan, who is the alchemical God of fire, and the patron of alchemy. When we see the Jewish tefillin, the black box over the third eye, it equates to a new world of wisdom through initiation, sexual energy. It incorporates the three prongs of shin, turning it into four.

The skull cap symbolises a 360 degree awareness. Incorrect or lustful emission of semen is given the term 'the synagogue of Satan', but anyone who transforms these forces correctly are given the title 'Lion of Judah'. In alchemy, Satan (Saturn) is the base metal and the Sun (Christ) is the gold of enlightenment. In alchemy, at the point of gold we become a solar vessel, known as 'the son of man' or Solomon, the Soliman, the solar man. The temple of Solomon is the mind. Solomon and the treasures of the temple mount is reference to knowledge within the mind. The song of Solomon (song of songs) is the Christ presence to the assembly of the elect. We sometimes borrow this light from the solar Sun which is the origin of lent, as it is light lent from the Sun, and we celebrate lent for 40 days which, again, has that magical spiritual number, the number 40.

Man is really the anti-Christ by the suppression of his own Christ within. Man is also made of carbon which has 6 protons, 6 electrons, and 6 neutrons = 666.

The bones of Christ, contrary to tradition at the time, were not broken. Saturn rules over bones and this is telling us that Satan/Saturn has no dominion over Christ. In sexual terms, lower sexual lust is a boner, which has relevance to Satanic consciousness.

Above Christ on the cross, you have the Latin letters INRI. INRI is Ignis Natura Renovatur Integra, meaning *"fire renews nature incessantly"* and this is the solar fire. Jesus supposedly died for our sins, but 'sin' in Greek is 'harmartia', meaning 'missing the mark'. This refers to an archery term for missing the centre gold bullseye so, in other words, when we miss our mark, our pineal gland of enlightenment, we are sinners. Those with knowledge, the Gnosis, are free from sin as they have not missed the mark. As it proclaims in Hosea 4:6, *"My people are destroyed for lack of knowledge"*.

Let he without sin cast the first stone. As I have previously mentioned, this means he without sin, the Gnostic with knowledge who has hit the mark of enlightenment, 'cast' which comes from the Hebrew word 'yadah/yada' which means 'know' or 'knowing' (knowledge), 'the first', first is the most important, 'stone' which is the foundation stone, and the stone of wisdom, the pineal gland. In other words, the Gnostic (Wiseman of knowledge) knows the knowledge of the stone. In this story, it talks about a prostitute being the subject. This, of course, takes us into lower sexual desire, which is satanic consciousness, hence why it is a story involving a prostitute, symbolising lower desire and immorality.

The famous holy trinity is the father who resides in the eye (pineal gland), the son who is the internal Christ who exists in everyone, and the Holy Spirit, or the dove (dove is greater knowledge), which is the fire of Kundalini. Jesus is the Lamb of God, and this is the Ram which is mind-light, illumination and Aries is the higher mind.

"I am the door of the sheep" – Jesus. Door is daleth, connected to daath which is the doorway to knowledge. Sheep symbolises waywardness of our divine knowledge. The lamb's blood on the door is the transmutation of Sulphur from Mercury, which is our alchemical ascension. It is the fire (sulphur) that we have to transmute in order to liberate this fire from our mercury by sexual energy and its usage to dissolve the ego. The blood is the river of the water of life that we must flow with at the path of least resistance to the Godhead (see Moses, parting of the red sea).

Now you know that our inner sexual energy is Christ, we can

now use this knowledge to translate The Lord's Prayer: The word 'prayer' derives from 'proseuche', which is a compound of the words *'pros'* and *'euche'*. The word *'pros'* is a preposition that means 'toward', and it can denote a sense of closeness. The word *'pros'* is used to portray the intimate relationship that exists between the members of the Godhead. The word *'euche'* is an old Greek word that describes a wish, desire, prayer, or a vow. Therefore, it is a wish or desire to reach the Godhead, which is a state of enlightenment.

The prayer position demonstrated by the hands is the number 10, 5+5, and this, again, gives us the decad of Pythagoras, the nine divisions of alchemy plus Azoth, the Christ fire.

"Our father" (abbas) – The satanic sexual energy (Saturn).

"Who art in heaven" – The Kundalini force raised to the highest chakras *(Heaven)*.

"Hallowed be thy name" – Ring of Saturn (halo) – (Ancient scholars said that to escape the lower Saturnalian desires was the path to Sainthood).

"Thy kingdom come, thy will be done, on Earth as it is in Heaven" – Generative sexual force, Earth = lower chakras, lower desire, and Heaven = higher chakras (7th chakra = 7th heaven).

"Give us this day, our daily bread" - Quintessence = Kundalini sexual energy which, in Sanskrit, is 'mana' (what Moses fed the Israelites during the Exodus).

Jesus stated *"I am the bread of life"* and 'Lord' means 'giver of bread'!

"Those who trespass against us" - To do something, or act in a

way, that is not morally acceptable, such as wasting the sacred seed (sperm/semen).

"And lead us not unto temptation" - Satanic lower sexual desires that tempt the initiates. Have better use of sexual energy, used with compassion (Christ) and not with passion/lust (Satan).

"Deliver us from evil" – Evil reversed is live. Live right and live now, live in the now as the Egyptians demonstrated with their Aker lions that symbolise yesterday and tomorrow. Enlightenment is in the eternal now. The red lion of lower Egypt represents the drinkable gold of alchemy and the white lion of upper Egypt is the secret fire (kundalini). Drinkable gold is aurum potabile and gold possess sun-like powers and therefore strengthens the sun force within. The hidden fire is the power to transform reality. The secret fire exists within the consciousness of the alchemist and that secret fire is kundalini. It is the serpentine working power within the body. Which can, once aroused into action, can destroy as it can create (Sodom and Gomorrah of the bible is symbolic of this). Only those who have gained the power to control their own self may be told how that power can be aroused in man. This secret fire is also symbolised by the sword/lance/arrows/javelin et al. It is also symbolised by the thunderbolts/lightning strike of Zeus and Jupiter. The scecret fire at its highest sense is thought or the Egyptian god Thoth and through intonation and vibration acts on matter to create new incarnations of the mind. This divine power is shared by humans on the power of inspired thought and imagination and this is one of the greatest secrets of the alchemist.

"For thine is the glory" – Thine is the solar force within us, the Krestos/Christ, the fire.

AMEN equals the number 33, which is the number of divine realisation. The word 'amen' is number 33 by its numerical value and alphabetical position. A=1, M= 13, E=5, N =14 = 33. The word 'amen' is from Ammon, the father God of Egypt, and was an Ancient Egyptian salutation to the supreme power of the universe. The Ancient Greek name Ammon (Aum-en or Aum-on) later becomes *"Amen"* in the Abrahamic religions. *"I am Alpha and Omega, the beginning and the end, the first and the last".* This would relate to Om being the last letter in the Greek alphabet, Omega meaning the *"great om"*.

The first syllable in Amen is 'Am', and is from the Greek 'Om', and it is also the Sanskrit mantra 'Om', written 'AUM' from the Hindu tradition. The word 'Om' is from the last word in the Greek alphabet Omega, which means the 'great om'. The Greek lowercase letter Omega, when turned to its side, looks very similar to the Sanskrit method of writing 'Om'. 'Om' is the Sanskrit 'Aum', which is the name of God. The second syllable in Amen is 'En', which can also be spelled as 'On' or 'Un'. The meaning of 'En' or 'On', is a state of being or power supply. It is through the Lord of the Thrones that we power on the light to illuminate our minds and the world around us. This is where we tap the internal fire to travel up Jacob's Ladder (spine) to the heavenly kingdom of Our Father (head/mind). Therefore, when you say *'Amen'* (AUM-On or AHM-On), you are saying the vibration of God, and are at a state of being with God or a source of Godly inspiration in which you are the conduit or power source.

Now, I am going to give you more examples that Christ is referring to our sexual force, our internal fire of enlightenment.

Jesus is a title meaning 'saviour', and 'saviour' means 'he who sows the seed', which is sperm. The word 'sperm' means 'seed'. Jesus starts his father's work aged 12, which is the age of puberty in male children. This is when they become sexually active with their fish of the sea, sperm, which is oiled by semen and becomes the anointed; 'anointed' means to 'oil'. Jesus was the only begotten son, but 'begotten' derives from 'mono-gene' which means 'one gene'. This is the one sperm that fertilises the egg (ovum). Jesus is the morning star, which is the planet Venus. In Sanskrit, 'Venus' is 'shukra', which means seminal or sexual secretion. Jesus is the morning star which has reference to sexual energy. Venus also gives us the word 'venereal'.

The word 'semen' derives from 'serere', which means 'to sow' which, again, comes back to 'seed' and 'saviour'. The retrograde of Venus lasts for 40 days and for 40 nights, ironically, the amount of time Jesus spent in the wilderness. Venus is symbolised by a shell, which is ego. The shell is Klipoth, known as the world of shells. Roman Catholic Popes sometimes wear a robe covered by shell symbols. Lucifer is also associated with the morning star and is sexual power, forming part of the Venustic initiation, which is the path of the middle or the middle path of balance.

(Robe of Shells)

Sperm not ejaculated enhances the sexual energy to be used in consciousness, transferring it upwards into the solar plexus (Bethlehem). 'Bethlehem' means 'house of bread', which is referring to the quintessence (Kundalini sexual energy) that I mentioned in The Lord's Prayer. This is the real origin of celibacy, sexual sublimation, retaining sexual energy, usually around 10% which gives us the origin of the meaning of tithing. John 3:4-10, *"whosoever is born god of god doth not commit sin, for his (seed remaineth in him)".* This is celibacy; retaining the seed and keeping it within you.

Many priests do not know the origin of celibacy and, for them, it has turned into sexual suppression, leading to criminal offences.

Jesus was baptised aged 30 which, again, has numerical and spiritual significance, as 30 is the number of the forces of spiritual enlightenment and connection to the supreme power. John the Baptist lost his head, and this is sperm detaching from its tail upon fertilisation. The baptism took place in the river Jordan; 'Jordan' means 'to descend' and it is the spinal fluid. Jordan runs into the Dead Sea, also known as the salt sea and, this, again, is spinal fluid which contains salt. The fifth initiation of the secret brotherhoods is called the Initiation of Ioannes (John) or the Revelation of John (John the Baptist).

This fifth level of initiation is the door to mastership and resurrection. Biblically, the dove then appears and descends above Christ who is in the river Jordan (descend), which illustrates enlightenment.

Baptism is the elevation from the waters below (Mayim) to the waters above (Shamayim/Heaven) poured over the crown chakra. The child symbolises the babies of initiation, the spiritually young in the teaching entering into that teaching. The symbolic cross on the head is the Ashen (Ash) cross. Egyptians wore an Ashen cross on the middle of their forehead, reminding them to keep secret the mysteries of their initiation. Christ crucified in Golgotha (Skull) is the secret teachings of the ages of the high priests, located in our brain, where it is allegorically killed and the mysteries hidden from the profane (uninitiated).

THE LAST SUPPER: THE MEANING

The Christ seed sits at the 'Mensa', meaning both 'table' and 'mind'. 'Supper' derives from 'soup', which means 'to consume liquid', which is DMT, and it is the last time that your mind will be under the influence of the false ego, which is the lower mind. The pineal gland naturally makes its own DMT, and a fundamental role of DMT in our consciousness is suggested by the brain's active transport of DMT into its confines, using precious energy. DMT is naturally produced by the pineal gland, transporting us to different states of mind and unimaginable realms of experience.

Dimethyltryptamine (DMT) is the liquid consumed (soup/supper) and it is the spiritual molecule. The now famous phrases of *eat my flesh is bread*, the quintessence and sexual Kundalini and *'drink my blood is wine'*, the wine of light which is transmuted semen that awakens the sacred fire, the alchemical elixir or life (eternal life). Christ sits between the 12 disciples, and 12 indicates the whole, or the end. Christ becomes the 13, the passage to a higher level and the number of eternal return and death from which there is transformation and resurrection, resurrection and transformation of self. The number 12 is used extensively within the Bible; in fact, 212 times.

For example:

12 Brothers of Israel

12 Brothers of Joseph

12 Judges of Israel

12 Great Patriarchs

12 Old Testament Prophets

12 Kings of Israel

12 Princesses of Israel

12 Jewels of the High Priest

12 Disciples of Christ

Women crowned with 12 stars

Holy city having 12 foundations

And so on.

DA VINCI'S LAST SUPPER CODES

'The Last Supper' is an iconic painting and also an iconic moment in religious history. In essence, 'supper' comes from 'soup' which means 'to consume liquid', which then takes us into DMT and the fluid of pineal gland enlightenment. Ironically, the organic compound structure of DMT is the indole ring, which is formed and adjoined by the pentagram and hexagram (5&6).

When we look at the painting, we also need to look at what is happening behind the characters because there is a lot going on. Each loaf of bread and each hand of the characters are a musical note, and the tablecloth shows a musical pentagram (yes, that word again). It gives us a 40 second piece of music from right to left, and the number 40 has deep biblical numerical and Kabbalistic significance.

(The Hands of Christ And The Disciples And The Bread Upon The Table Are Musical Notes – Right To Left)

It was discovered by Italian musician Giovanni Maria Pala, and is a 40 second requiem, a hymn to God from right to left, which is how Da Vinci for the most part wrote, backwards.

Whichever way you count, Christ is the centre, the number 7, with 6 disciples each side of him, giving us the number 13 which, as stated, is the passage to a higher level, the eternal return. The number 13 is death, from which there is transformation and resurrection of a new self.

The 7th note is middle F, which equals 349 hertz in frequency. What is the relevance of 349?

In the Bible, the word 'saviour' is used 349 times, and 'saviour' means 'he who sows the seed'; the seed is male sperm (again, this has deep relevance to Christ). The act of the foot washing that Christ conducted prior to his crucifixion symbolises that the Christ within is actually our loving servant.

There are 11 windows visible in the painting and 13, which is the number of people present, divided by 11 = 1.18.

In Corinthians 1.18, it states, *"What is hidden or secret can be revealed by God's Spirit (Fire of Kundalini) He makes evident those things we need to know but for those who have refused to repent (Pent = Pentagram) and humble themselves, he will not give them his Spirit and without his Spirit, they cannot ever understand the mystery of the gospel"*.

In Greek (Corinth), a mystery is a secret impossible to penetrate; that which is crystal clear to those on the inside is unintelligible to those who are on the outside. The initiates know what the vulgar (unsophisticated/uninitiated) do not know.

The numerical value of LEONARDO DA VINCI is 1610, which is also the value of *'Easter Sunday'*. The egg is symbolic of the secret of being, the innermost that we find by working through the closed shell.

The egg is also the sexual energy/force of the man and woman transmuted through the sexual act, where the sperm and ovum are transformed into energy. This, of course, then takes us back to the saviour and seed! This could then also take us into the Oval Office within the White House of Washington DC; oval is the egg.

GOLGOTHA – THE PLACE OF SKULLS

'Golgotha' means 'the place of skulls', and this is referring to the head, where wisdom illuminates us. It is where we get the light to become enlightened. Golgotha is also the biblical walls of Jericho, which means 'city of the moon', as the skull encases the semi lunar-ganglion and lunar is the moon. Within our minds, there are always two choices, and this is our doubting Thomas, whose real name was Didymus which means twin, namely 'duality', which causes a lack of a union of self and causes separation. Doubting, as in doubting Thomas, is double-mindedness which is the twin, our duality. In other words, two minds.

Jesus said to St Peter, *"Before the Rooster crows you will deny me three times"*. This is really referring to the three stages of the initiation path, as in the three days in the tomb, etc., but more on this soon. A rooster is associated with the Holy Spirit, the phoenix, and awakening of Kundalini. He was betrayed by Judas, but Judas derives from the Hebrew 'Judah', which connects to the Hebrew words Daleth (doorway) and Daath (knowledge), therefore Judas is the doorway to knowledge and it leads us to the Christ. Judas is the dissolution of ego. Judas therefore leads us to the Christ just as Judas led the authorities to Christ before his Earthly demise.

The double cross is the symbol of sulphur, the male principle that acts with mercury (female) to create all metals. It is the manifestation of the will of Heaven. Anger and hate is the alchemical Hell, the sulphur released within our chemical makeup with these emotions, whereas love and acceptance is alchemical Heaven through the genetic waters of our DNA. Water is the symbol of wisdom. Water and fish feature numerous times in the Bible. Jesus is the fisher of men, and fish are the initiates awakened in the water as alchemical purification is done through the water within our DNA. This is an inner alchemical process. The mermaid/merman is symbolic of such transformation. The Pope's mitre fish hat is also relevant to this.

(Alchemical Symbol of Sulphur – The Fire and Brimstone of Hell)

Now Jesus was placed between the two thieves, and this is known as the three crosses on Calvary in Golgotha. The three crosses are the three ways of seeing, namely monism, dualism, and non-duality, which is a mature state of consciousness without division or conflict. Now we get more numerology as we move on with the story.

Jesus died aged 33 in 33AD, and 33 is the number of divine realisation, hence why it is encrypted within this aspect of the Christ story. 33 is a master number and, biblically, it is used several times.

For example, Jacob had 33 sons and ruled Israel for 7 years, which are the 7 chakras that are situated within the spine, the human spine is the famous Jacob's Ladder. On the 33rd biblical mention of Jacob, it refers to Jacob's Ladder, which has 33 vertebrae. This leads back to Atlantis, too. The number 33 is also relevant in freemasonry, as the highest level publically known is 33 degrees.

33 also has relevance to DNA, as you will now see.

Human language is a reflection of inherent DNA, and the alkaline within DNA follows a law of grammar. Verbal words are genetic expressions manifesting through our vocal cords. Words are genetics and words can alter genes. And, by the misuse of words, we are misusing our fifth chakra which contains our Adam's Apple. It is the fall of man within Eden (Eden = the body).

We are a 3 billion letter genetic code, which is deciphered by our hyaluronic acids, and we are a genetic language. This figure does not take into account the countless genetics science calls 'junk DNA', which is really a protein-based coded language yet to be activated. With a shift in consciousness, we change our code. DNA is a living data storage containing instructions for our greater potential.

DNA and RNA are 2 polarities of consciousness; RNA is an 'A' form helix and DNA is a 'B' form helix. One strand is positive and one strand is negative, due to unparalleled twists. The universe sees both positive and negative as equal, a parity and this is the basis of duality. Even in mathematics we can demonstrate this, 2 is a positive and -2 is a negative and this can be done with any number. Numbers are however merely what we use as symbols to represent a certain equasion. If I were to write number 10, for example, on a chalkboard and then remove it the number 10 doesn't disappear from the universe because the number I have written is purely representative of that numeric, it is not the number itself. Duality are 2 separate parts of self, the immortal being of light (spirit/soul) and the mortal darkenss (flesh/materiality) which is yin and yang which was later adapted by Christianity as good and evil. It is the two opposing forces that are an inherent part of human nature and they are in constant battle for control.

The two strands of our double helix DNA twist in opposite directions until the 11th twist, when they then twist the opposite way and then on the next 11th twist, they twist again, and then on the next 11th twist, they twist again, until we get to the number 33 which completes the DNA sequence.

This gives us 11:11:11 (33), which is why it is said that 11:11:11 is a DNA activation code.

DNA is also the hidden message within the Sumerian Annunaki story, written as a metaphor for our higher potential or, as the Egyptians phrased it, a higher type of human.

The biblical Enoch is relevant, as 'Enoch' means 'dedication', and it is this dedication that will drive us to illuminate the mind. The Greek word 'phoenix', as in 'phoenix from the flames', is a reference to awakened consciousness through Kundalini fire and it derives from the Egyptian word 'Pa-Hanok' meaning *'House of Enoch'* with house being a synonym of mind. The mind is the place where we get the light to become enlightened. Most people go through life never knowing that they are a universe in miniature. The number 33 is highly relevant. The number 11, which leads us to 33, is the Arcanum 11, which is man and woman as the two columns.

Our spiritual journey ends with full spiritual enlightenment, which is symbolised by the crown of thorns, and full spiritual enlightenment is code for the Son of God.

Before his arrest in the Garden of Gethsemane, Jesus prayed three times and, as stated in the last chapter, between the sixth hour (Temptation) and the ninth hour (Sexual Magic), the initiate enters into the crucifixion of his spiritual night. 'Gethsemane', amongst other things, means 'press of the eight'. 7+1=8, and 7 indicates the end in order to become 8, which is the octave. The 8th note is a new cycle at a higher level and is also therefore associated with the number one as a new beginning. In the biblical number, 8 means resurrection and new beginnings. 888 is the numerical value of Jesus in Greek Gemetria, and it takes 8 minutes for the light of the Sun to reach Earth, the Sun being the cosmic Christ. In the next passage, it is the number 8 that is numerically important.

Jesus resurrected on the first day, which is the 8th day, the first day of a new cycle at a higher level. He was not recognised by Mary Magdalene, as he had transmuted. This is the transition from the 7th octave to the 8th, and it is the 7 stages of alchemical transformation which is the alpha and omega, the beginning and the end. The empty tomb is Plato's cave, meaning to escape ignorance and darkness with an ascent into the true light (Christ). The cave means to be cut off from the true light. Three days in the tomb is symbolic of the 3 woes (Initiation).

DAY 1 is the ninth sphere; the belly of the whale, the temple of Jerusalem where you build your own temple twice. The temple of Jerusalem was said to have been built twice.

DAY 2 is Geburah; the energy that makes way for the new, penetrates the initiate, and destroys ego to become the resurrected master of light and fire.

DAY 3 is penetration into the mysteries and transformation out of the belly of the whale, into light – ending the 3 initiation days!

This is, of course, the meaning of Jonah and the whale. Jonah is the pineal gland and the whale is Malkuth, the body. The three days of darkness in Egypt, during the 10 plagues, also has this meaning.

'Resurrection' means 'to use again', which is reference to sexual sublimation and the re-use of sexual energy.

THE MIRACLES OF CHRIST: ARE NOT REAL EVENTS

When Christ walked on water in Galilee, it was a metaphor. 'Galilee' derives from the feminine noun 'Gulgoleth', meaning head/skull (Golgotha), and the masculine noun 'Gilgal' meaning 'wheel', which is a symbol of higher consciousness. This relates to the biblical chariot in the sky and also the biblical wheel in the vision of Ezekiel. 'Gilgal' gives us Google, the modern day search engine of knowledge.

It is symbolic of being above the water in an elevated state.

When Christ fed the 5000 with five loaves and two fish, this was also metaphorical. It makes little sense to physically be able to do this and share such little food with a mass gathering. The two fish refer to the higher and lower consciousness of Pisces, the two fish of the zodiac, facing upwards and downwards.

(Zodiac Sign of Pisces - Two Fishes)

Loaves are linked to the wheat of Virgo. 'Virgo' is Latin for 'virgin' and the virgin, Virgo in the zodiac, has a shaft of wheat. This is virgin consciousness and is a place of no thought in a state of meditation. This is where the 'bread', or truth of the virgin, is consumed. Virgin consciousness can be described as 'meditation starts when thought stops'. Bread also has relevance to quintessence, as previously stated, which refers to Kundalini and activated consciousness through the pineal gland. The number five, as in five loaves, also refers to consciousness as a fifth element, the ether, and the pentagram.

We can conclude that the ability of God to enlighten man is unlimited. The story uses numbers to convey the meaning of the story. We start with virgin consciousness (an empty mind) to allow divine intervention/spirit/the light to act and achieve perfection as we unite with God. The 12 baskets of leftovers means this, 12 is cosmic order and completion, a basket is symbolic of everything made divine, but can also mean the womb and fertility which has Moses connotations with the basket in the water, referring to the womb and fertility. A basket that is empty is a metaphor for an unconsciousness mind, therefore, if the basket was full of leftovers, it means the opposite, a mind that is conscious. So the multitudes are really fed spiritually, not physically.

Turning water into wine is code for the water of life (semen) transmuted into the wine of light (transmuted semen) that awakens the sacred fire. This miracle occurred at the wedding of Cana which is a place in Galilee, the head/mind, which is the place of consciousness.

But, first of all, we need to unblock our 7 chakras, which is Christ cleansing the 7 unclean spirits, allowing the Kundalini energy to travel from Earth to Heaven within the body. The 7 chakras are also the 7 candle sticks that Christ walked amongst. With all this complete, we see the rapture of Christ which means 'transition'; it is the transition of our self and we become the good shepherd, the enlightened. Our seat of enlightenment, the pineal gland, secretes a white and brown substance during this process and this is code for the biblical land of Milk and Honey.

By now, the initiate has activated the Ark of the Covenant, which is the brain. The cherubims are the two hemispheres of the brain, and a symbol of the spiritually enlightened person. It is the fountain of wisdom and the mercy seat of all stages of initiation, the initiates of the flame in the brain of man.

(Ark of the Covenant)

So there you are, Christ was not a physical man, Christ is our inner illumination that we can activate by using the correct use of our sexual forces. And, with that said, each and every one of us is Christ in waiting. We have been taught and, in many cases, brainwashed into believing in an outside saviour, when all along that saviour was within us. You have to admit that it has been a great mechanism and an ingenious plan that has lasted for thousands of years. Christ is not coming out of the clouds on a white horse. A white horse was used as it is a metaphor for a higher mind and a higher connection, hence why there are numerous white chalk horses carved into hills around the UK. The four horsemen of the apocalypse are not coming either. They, too, are metaphors, as you saw earlier in the book. Do not fear Hell as it is not a real place, and do not fear a vengeful God as that is a creation of man.

Now is the time to know the truth.

This follows on to other famous biblical characters and stories and, in the following chapters, I will show you how.

NINE

THE CHURCH AND MARY MAGDALENE: THE TWO BRIDES OF CHRIST

As you approach a church, you cannot miss the wonderful sacred geometry within its design and, if you are anything like me, you marvel at its greatness. But this geometry was not just there for aesthetic reasons, it goes deeper. Frequency plays a big part in consciousness, and this is why ancient sites, such as Stonehenge and the Giza pyramids, were resonance chambers. Resonance structures have a wavelength of pure consciousness, creating a tri-thalamic entrainment frequency. This is why we have such frequencies as the Solfeggio scale, which are voice harmonies of ancient monasteries and are tones that impart spiritual blessings. It gave the sound of sanctity, and this opened up inner portals of wisdom, becoming a route to enlightenment. 'Cathedral' means 'seat', which is referring to the seat of consciousness, the pineal gland, and 'bishop' comes from the word 'watcher', which means 'awake' or 'he who is awake'. *Thine is the glory'* and thine is code for the solar force within us (Krestos/Christ fire).

Churches and sacred buildings were made to the proportions of man, known as the *cannon*. It was an ancient proverb that to know thyself is to know the universe. We are, in fact, the universe in miniature. As I have previously mentioned, the word 'church' derives from 'Circe', which derives from 'circle'. This is where sacred geometry, again, makes an appearance.

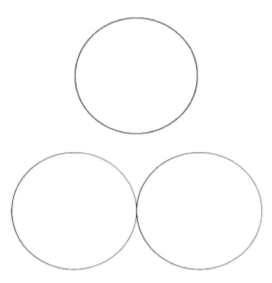

(One circle gives us oneness, and a circle beside a circle indicates the separation into duality.)

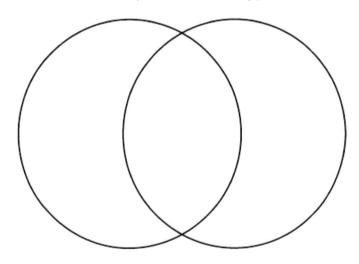

(When we interlink the two circles, we get the vesical Pisces.)

This now nicely leads us on to the next aspect of the chapter.

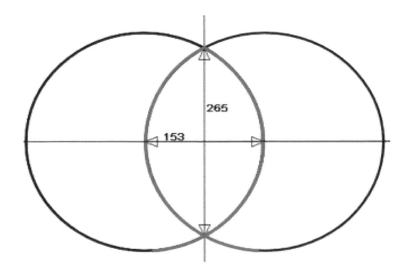

(153 contained within the Vesica Pisces.)

Within the Vesica Pisces, in the Mandorla meaning 'almond', we get that number 153 again. Cast your mind back to the Egyptian section with the entrance of the Great Pyramid being at the seventeenth course level, and many more examples of 153 within the Great Pyramid and Giza itself. 153 is the number of the master and divine knowledge. It just so happens that the ministry of Jesus lasted 153 weeks and, after his resurrection, he caught exactly 153 fish with his disciples. It is a hidden numerical message. The net was cast on the right–hand side of the boat, which indicates the right-brain.

When we translate the name 'Mary Magdalene' into Greek (η αγδαληνή), it has a numerical value of 153. This tells us that Mary Magdalene is the yoni and the doorway to life, the doorway to Eden. The yoni/womb is the true identity of the Holy Grail. The word 'grail' derives from 'Graal', which means 'Vessel *of God'*. And the product of that chalice/cup is the child. Between the endocervix and the ectocervix of the womb, we have the region known as the transformation zone, and it is said that those who drink from the grail spiritually transform. Biblically the matrix is the womb which is symbolised by the vesica piscis and the number 153. It is the Yoni, the gateway to life after 9 months in the womb (that sacred number 9 again).

The shape of this region resembles the chalice. The red wine in the chalice is menstrual blood, known as the soma (drink) of the mystics. Menstrual blood transports you to endocrine state of rapture (third eye awakening). Rapture, also as in the rapture of Christ, means transformation.

It was a ritual which derives from RTU (menses), which means 'menstrual cycle' in Sanskrit. Monday 22nd July is the day of the Feast of Mary Magdalene, occurring on the same date each year. The date 22nd July gives us the mathematical formula of 22/7, which is an abbreviated shorthand way of writing pi, just as we write 24/7 for 24 hours a day, 7 days a week. 153 also gives us that coded message again of 9. 1+5+3=9. The first digits of PI are 3.141 and this also equals 9. PI as a circle is 360 degrees and that gives us 3+6+0=9.

When the alphabet is split into 2 symmetrical sections (A-M and N-Z) the central pillar is the number 7 = G. By adding the prime numbers on both sides, we get 22. 22/7 (Central Pillar 7) = 22/7 = pi as the tetragrammaton of the name Yahweh (YHWH) which is 26 in Gemetria. There are 26 letters of the English alphabet. The central pillar is the G within the masonic compass. The G is gnosis (knowledge).

(The alphabet split into 2 symmetrical sections.)

Pi is the circle which gives us the word 'Circe', which gives us the word 'church'. The most prominent circle in nature is the Sun, which is the cosmic Christ.

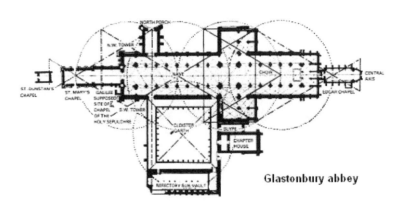

(Glastonbury Abbey)

The likes of Glastonbury Abbey, and others, are designed as a continuous Vesica Piscis, which is the Ad-Triangulum, meaning 'of the triangle'. This, of course, takes us back to the alchemical law of the triangle, with its three essences of sulphur, mercury, and salt.

Mary Magdalene gives a proclamation of the teachings of Christ 83 times and, in Hebrew, Bread = 83. Bread is quintessence, which is Kundalini sexual energy (A.K.A. Mana, the bread fed to the Israelites by Moses). In sexual terms, the union of opposites takes place in the bridal chamber, which is code for attaining Christhood, the alchemical marriage, mystery union of Christ and Mary Magdalene which, in Ancient Egypt, was known as 'tying the knot'. The commandment of *honour your father and your mother* is telling us to honour the divinity of our own polar opposites.

Now back to the church. Most church arches are Lunette arches which means 'Moon' (lunar).

(Lunette Arch)

The lunette arch is female genitalia, the four gates of the vagina. It is the entrance of the yoni (Mary Magdalene), the entrance to the church. As you enter the church, you get taken through the human chakra system, from the root through to the crown, as you walk up the aisle. In church, we also have hymns, which derives from who was also the Greek God of Weddings. A chorus originally meant dance in a circle (circle – Circe – church). When you look at the likes of the famous Glastonbury Abbey and many others, you see that its design contains a continuous Vesica Piscis called Ad Triangulum, which is Latin for *'of the triangle'*, meaning an equilateral triangle.

White, as in the usual colour of a wedding dress, means an alchemical marriage of opposites, male/female Earth/Heaven and so on.

DA VINCI'S CODE:

MONA LISA: Christ and Magdalene

Even the famous Mona Lisa painting contains this esoteric message of divine opposites. Mona is Madonna (no coincidence with the 80s pop sensation), and gives us the phrase 'Our Lady'.

Lisa derives from 'L'isa' and 'Isa' is 'Jesus' in Arabic, but Jesus never existed as a man, so what does it mean?

People often comment on the androgyny of the painting, and this is because Da Vinci was telling us of the Union of opposites, masculine and feminine. Most people think that 'our lady' refers to Mother Mary, however, original Latin associates this title with Mary Magdalene, the bride of Christ. Mary Magdalene and Jesus were considered equals, and this is why we have the androgynous image we call the Mona Lisa, the Magdalene, and the Christ. The numbers 5 and 6 have been clearly hidden either side of Lisa's shoulders, and the position of her hands also gives us the symbology of 5 and 6 in, what is known as, the 'Polaris Diagram'.

(The Mona Lisa)

Behind her, in the archway, better seen on more enhanced pictures, we are shown the number 72 which relates to several esoteric things, such as Iod-Hei-Vav-Hei which, numerically, is 72. This is the numerical value of God in Hebrew. It is also the numbers of letters in the three main languages of the Bible, Hebrew (22), Greek (24), and English (26), and therefore the conveyance of the divine message. Vav is also the bridge (between Man and God) and, in this painting, the number 72 is located beneath an arched bridge.

Mary Magdalene is the vessel of God, the Yoni which contains the Holy Grail, the womb. The Church and Mary Magdalene are both referred to as *the bride of Christ.*

TEN

MOSES:
THE JOURNEY OF ENLIGHTENMENT

We all know the biblical version of Moses, so I won't recite it again here. Instead, I will break down the main factors of the story, piece by piece, to show you their real meanings.

Moses was found in a basket, or so we're told, by Egyptian royalty and brought up in high society. You all know the biblical version of the story but, in this chapter, you are going to hear the deeper esoteric meaning of the story and what it was originally teaching us. Moses is a metaphor. Moses, deriving from 'Moshe', meaning 'born of water and fire', represents the Thelema, which is the spiritual will and spiritual power of our own God within. Moses is our illuminated mind through spiritual will, the deliverer.

Through Moses, we attain union of Israel, the Promised Land which, contrary to popular belief, is not a physical place, it is an enlightened state. The New Jerusalem of the book of Revelation is code for Christ consciousness. Israel is what it is to be the perfect spiritual man (not that the nation acts that way) and we can see this by separating the word; Is (Isis) RA (Sun/Male) and EL (God). It is the union of man-woman-God. When IS becomes purified, the RA incarnates through chastity into the human being (Christ force), known as the ISRA. ISRA is the two parts of EL (God) and is the union of opposites with the divine.

The burning bush on Mount Sinai is the pineal gland activated by Kundalini spiritual fire, often symbolised by the Acacia tree that contains DMT. The brazen (brass) serpent which Moses used to free the Israelites from captivity was originally bronze, which is a combination of two metals, namely copper and tin, which gives us male-female. Unite them in fire and you make the third force bronze, this is the serpent of bronze. This is the serpent at the base of the spine, Kundalini. In the Kabballah, Egypt is the Klipoth, the abyss where sexual energy is stored, the lower chakras. This is the biblical captivity from where we must exodus, and exodus means the way out, it is from where we must find the way out. By freeing the soul by magnum opus (great work), it leads to the transmutation of the body into an illuminated being (philosopher's stone).

When Moses parted the water, it was again metaphorical. Water is the way and the path of least resistance to our Godhead. In Alchemy, this is referred to as an *open sea or the sea of the wise*. The story of Exodus is in three verses (19, 20, 21) and each verse contains 72 letters which, as previously stated, is God and the transmission of the sacred message. Out of the red sea and into the wilderness then into the Promised Land is metaphorical for taking us from unconsciousness to enlightenment and our Moses (Moshe), our spiritual determination, leads the way. They spent 40 years in the wilderness, because the number 40 has the power and energy to transform you to a spiritual state. The staff of Moses is the human spine that acts as a conduit between the body and mind, and the serpent of Moses that devoured the serpents of the magicians of the Pharaoh indicates a superior knowledge of occult powers - occult means hidden - and it is the ability to override the physical world, the four.

The 10 commandments are what is needed to extricate (free) ourselves from the currents of the left-hand path (loss of consciousness) and to the right-hand path (Godhead), known as turning the coin of self. This is the origin of flipping a coin to make a decision whereby, here in the UK, we say heads or tails; in other words heads, enlightenment, or tails, the Klipoth, the devil's tail, the Kundabuffer, that leads you to a downward spiral into the abyss.

And why 10? As previously stated, each of the three essences of alchemy contain the other two, giving us 3x3 which are the nine divisions. The number 10, the Azoth, is the decad of Pythagoras, the eternal fire, illustrated by the burning bush.

Moses received the law of God at Sinai, and the Hebrew word for 'receive' is 'kibel'. The word 'kibel' gives us the root word of Kabballah, which are the mystical teachings of Judaism but, in order to receive, you must be receptive. A mountain is a metaphor for a place of revelation where, due to its height, we are closer to God. To go to the mountain means dedication to spiritual life.

THE 10 COMMANDMENTS: AND THEIR MEANINGS

"Thou shalt have no other gods before me"

This really means worship yourself, for you are divine. Me, in the Kabballah, is code for God, which is you.

"Thou shalt not make unto thee any graven image or any likeness of anything that is in heaven above, or that is in the earth beneath, or that is in the water under the earth"

This speaks of idol worship on the surface, but we can definitely go deeper. Materialism is one aspect of idol worship; the worship of a person and the satisfaction you get from the approval of that person. People can worship their problems, wallowing in anger and dissatisfaction. These are all examples of bowing down to graven images.

"Thou shalt not take the name of the Lord thy God in vain"

In other words, never ever put yourself down or think that you are somehow less deserving than anybody else. The "I AM" within you is strong.

The word *"vain"* means, among other things, *"no value"*. Never think of yourself as unworthy, because *"you are the light of the world"*.

"Remember the Sabbath day, to keep it holy"

The word "Sabbath", metaphysically, means *"seven"*, which is symbolic of spiritual completion and the seventh chakra (crown), enlightenment. The Sabbath is a state of mind, not a day of the week to not do any work. The seventh day means the seventh or perfect stage of one's spiritual unfoldment. Man has become so lost in the darkness of sense consciousness and has to reverse this trend in order to save himself.

When man becomes so at one with the father-mind as to feel it consciously, he also recognises this eternal peace in which all things are accomplished.

"Honour thy father and thy mother"

This is your own inner duality that must be unified as one to take you into non-duality, which is oneness. It is telling you to honour your own inner polarities and to bring them into unity and balance.

"Thou shalt not kill"

Metaphorically, this is referring to the kill, and that is to kill the soul out of a person. The likes of the Pharisees, meaning *"dividers"*, are telling people not to go within themselves, therefore denying them access to the Kingdom. *The kingdom of god is within you*, remember that, to go outside of self is to deny God's Kingdom, which is within YOU.

"Thou shalt not commit adultery"

This refers to intimate sexual knowledge, telling you to not waste the sacred seed of creation. The seed placed from Kundalini transforms into the virgin birth within you. The child of promise has been conceived through the marriage of mind and spirit. This is talking about a deep connection with the higher self, a very intimate, very personal, deep connection within you. If you are attempting to commune with the higher by using the lower, you are committing adultery.

"Thou shalt not steal"

The gifts within you have been stolen and hidden deep within you by the very people that say that they are trying to save your soul. The ones that interpreted the Bible incorrectly have stolen from you. They have stolen the sacred knowledge that will raise your very being to sanctity. They have taken away the key of knowledge from you.

"Thou shalt not bear false witness against thy neighbour"

Metaphysically speaking, the word 'neighbour' means something that is very close to you in an inner sense, within you. It is an inner being that is a part of you, so you must not bear false witness, and you must not lie or tell an untruth about your higher nature. Spiritual wisdom is your neighbour and it's a sacred holy part of you. For example, if someone tells you that you will touch something evil in your mind by meditating, that's bearing false witness against your neighbour.

"Thou shalt not covet thy neighbour's house - thou shalt not covet thy neighbour's wife, nor his manservant, nor his maidservant, nor his ox, nor his ass, nor anything that is thy neighbour's"

To covet your neighbour's wife means that you are living in the emotions. Female is spirit in the higher, and emotion in the lower. Coveting is a lower aspect. Coveting your neighbour's house is to live from the carnal mind. The ox and the ass are the power of the lower nature. The power of the mind is the ox, and the stubborn nature of the mind is the ass. Relying on your strong stubborn nature to lead your life is coveting the ox and ass. And biblically, when Christ rides the ass, the Christ assumes dominion over the stubborn nature, riding and steering it into Jerusalem, the higher realms of consciousness within you. The staff of Moses is the human spine, which is a conduit between the body and the mind. The serpent is the symbol of wisdom and, of course, contains the word 'pent' which is 'five', the ether. The staff of the priests is called the 'serpent crosier'. The crown shown below is the symbol of mastery and the union that takes place within the student when the life forces are lifted to the brain and they become the masters of wisdom. All initiates into the sacred mysteries are called Nagas, or Serpents of Wisdom. The serpent is the vehicle to messianic consciousness.

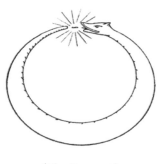

(The Serpent)

All of these commandments come into harmony when you go within yourself, and this is the real esoteric meaning of the 10 commandments, with 'ment' meaning mind.

THE 10 PLAGUES:

The 10 plagues of Egypt are no different, and are really referring to an inner spiritual process of enlightenment. The 10 plagues (as told in the Bible):

(1) Blood
(2) Frogs
(3) Lice
(4) Flies
(5) Pestilence of cattle
(6) Boils
(7) Hail
(8) Locusts
(9) 3 days of darkness
(10) Death of the firstborn

So, let's analyse what the story is telling us.

In the Kabbalah, the children of Israel (a term for the Israelites) were kept in Egypt in captivity. But, in the Kabbalah, Egypt is the section of the body from the kidneys downwards, the sacral chakra. Israel is a metaphor, as stated, for the perfect spiritual man, IS (Isis/Feminine aspect of self) RA (Sun/Male aspect of self), and EL which is God. Therefore, it is the balance of opposites with God; the perfect spiritual state.

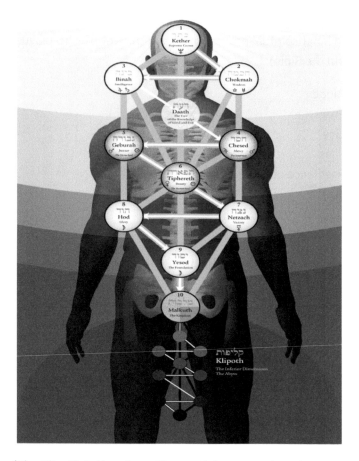

(The Klipoth is the abyss, the captivity – seen here between the legs)

Therefore, the story tells us of the exodus, meaning 'the way' or 'the road out', between the lower aspects of self and the higher aspects of self; the journey from Egypt to Israel.

Moses released the Israelites through the rise of the 'brazen serpent', which is really Kundalini awakening that goes from deactivation at the base of the spine to the mind, the upper chakras (Heaven) through various spiritual practices. Kundalini is the serpent of fire within us.

The 10 plagues are metaphorical of this inner journey that transitions us from Egypt to Israel. The dispute between Moses and the Pharaoh is the dispute between the illuminated mind (Moses) and the Pharaoh, in this story, representing the ego that we must battle with and overcome.

So now let's break down the 10 plagues:

Blood has regenerative properties and can transition you to a spiritual man (or woman). The frog is symbolic of easy transition, as a frog does between earth and water. Also, a symbol of regeneration, and the amulet of the frog is associated with resurrection. Lice are symbolic of external man (the senses). Flies are symbolic of death (death of the old you). Pestilence of cattle is symbolic of good acquired through truth. Boils relate to the skin and, in Hebrew, 'skin' is the same word as 'light'. In other words, skin is either a separator or a connector between self and others.

It can be either a divider or a unifying force. Hail is symbolic of falsity destroying truth. Locusts are symbolic of great numbers (those who make the transition during the exodus) into Israel, to become perfected spiritual man, and grasshopper/locust symbolises the freedom, independence, and enlightenment that will come as a result of listening to our hearts and making mindful decisions toward progress. After all, the grasshopper only jumps forward, never backward.

Darkness represents ignorance and falsity of true light and, as with Jonah in the belly of the whale for three days and Jesus in the tomb for three days, it has relevance to the initiation process, which I will go into in the Christ chapter.

And death of the firstborn refers to the death of spiritual darkness and the coming into spiritual light, which is knowledge and wisdom. When initiates have passed their initiation, they are referred to as the 'twice born', the born again, which first requires the death of their own firstborn! No-one can see the kingdom of God unless they are born again.

The whole story represents the inner spiritual journey from one of captivity to one of enlightenment lead by Moses, our illuminated mind.

In 70 years of excavations, archaeologists in the region of the exodus have found no physical evidence of an estimated 600,000 to 2.4 million people transiting through the desert. And yet, we can find dinosaur bones from 65 million years ago! There is good reason for the lack of physical evidence; it didn't physically happen, it is a metaphor for our own inner spiritual journey from darkness to light, from ignorance to enlightenment through the open sea, the path of least resistance.

The exodus happened within us, and it happens within every person who comes into the Gnosis and through the initiate taught in that Gnosis.

Your Moses can lead the way and can feed you your Mana bread, the quintessence of sexual force that illuminates the mind and releases you from the captivity of your lower self with the activation of your Kundalini (brazen serpent).

You, too, can take the path of least resistance, the open sea, into the Promised Land which is your own enlightenment by overcoming your own ego (Pharaoh). This is the true meaning of the Moses story.

ELEVEN

NOAH AND THE ARCANUM

According to the Bible, God saw how great wickedness had become and decided to wipe humankind off the face of the Earth. But one righteous man among all the people of that time, Noah, found favour in God's eyes.

With very specific instructions, God told Noah to build an ark for him and his family in preparation for a catastrophic flood that would destroy every living thing on Earth. God also instructed Noah to bring into the ark two of all living creatures, both male and female, and seven pairs of all the clean animals, along with every kind of food to be stored for the animals and his family while on the ark. Noah obeyed everything God commanded him to do.

After Noah and his family had entered the ark, rain fell for a period of forty days and nights. The waters flooded the Earth for a hundred and fifty days, and every living thing was destroyed.

As the waters receded, the ark came to rest on the mountains of Arafat. Noah and his family continued to wait for almost eight more months while the surface of the Earth dried out.

Finally, after an entire year, God invited Noah to come out of the ark. Immediately, Noah built an altar and offered burnt sacrifices with some of the clean animals to give thanks to God for deliverance. God was pleased with the offerings and promised never again to destroy all the living creatures as he had just done.

Later, God established a covenant with Noah: "*Never again will there be a flood to destroy the earth*". As a sign of this everlasting covenant, God set a rainbow in the clouds. Noah was the grandson of Methuselah, the oldest person in the Bible, who died at 969 years old in the year of the flood. Noah's father was Lamech, but we are not told his mother's name. Noah was a tenth generation descendant of Adam, the first human being on Earth.

Scripture tells us Noah was a farmer (Genesis 9:20). He was already 500 years old when he fathered three sons: Shem, Ham, and Japheth. Noah lived 350 years after the flood and died at 950 years old.

God's purpose in the flood was not to destroy people, but to destroy wickedness and sin. Before God decided to wipe the people from the face of the Earth, he first warned Noah, making a covenant to save Noah and his family. The whole time, Noah and his family laboured constantly to build the ark (120 years), and he also preached a message of repentance. With the coming judgment, God provided plenty of time and a way of escape for those who would look to him in faith. But the violent generation ignored Noah's message.

Noah's story is said to serve as an example of righteous living and enduring faith in the face of completely immoral and faithless times.

But did Noah really spend 120 years of his life building a wooden ark for two of every animal to escape the great flood, penguins waddling from Antarctica to the Middle East trying to get there in time, thankfully making it?

It is now the year 2019, and do people still believe there was once a wooden ark that housed many thousands of animals, avoiding a gigantic global flood hundreds of years in planning?

Genesis 7:10, *"and it came to pass after seven days that the waters of the flood were upon the earth".*

After the 7th chakra is reached and the Kundalini raises, the flood is upon us, that being the flood of spiritual energy, coming to rest on the mountain of Arafat. 'Arafat' means 'high ground' or 'sacred land', which are the higher realms of consciousness within us.

The story is a metaphor for the wonder that is creation, the amalgamation of the sacred fishes of the sea, sperm, and the ovum. Fish are a symbol of the initiates who have awakened in the water. It is code for alchemical purification which is done through the water of our DNA. It is an internal alchemical process. Rain is the creative sexual energy that comes from Heaven. The number 40 in numerology has the power to take you to a spiritual state. It rained for 40 days and 40 nights!

At the time of the biblical flood, as dated by the Bible, the date of the flood as beginning 2345 BCE and ending in 2344 BCE, there were ancient civilisations who continued their lives in their part of the world and made no mention of a global flood.

The city of Ur of the Chaldees (Ancient Sumer, location of the "plains of Shinar", hangout of Noah) was the leading city from about 2400 BCE until about 2285 BCE, and its history is not broken by any flood in this period.

Babylon was rising to power from about 2400 BCE on and reached a great height of civilisation under the famous King Hammurabi, who would have been a contemporary of Hebrew patriarch Abraham (about 2250 BCE) and, again, there is no break in this history due to a flood.

In Egypt, the 5th Dynasty, which began to reign about 2465 BCE, was followed by the 6th Dynasty (2323 BCE), which ruled to about 2000 BCE. This time period is very well-documented and there was no disruption during the 5th Dynasty at the time of Noah's flood, 2345 BCE, with the nation remaining strong and powerful throughout these dynasties.

The Harappan Civilisation (2300-1900 BCE) in India shows no disruptions at the time of the flood and, ironically, appears to have ended because of a region-wide drought! Chinese history begins nearly 3000 BCE. The Shu-King historic record of China shows that King Yao came to the throne in 2356 BCE and ruled China for many years after the alleged flood. Incidentally, during the reign of Yao, the Shu King reports that the Hwang Ho River flooded on a number of times, for three generations, again, with NO break in history. The only place you find these early rulers listed are at Chinese sites (spelled Tangyao, Westerners shorten this to Yao).

Ancient civilisations in India, which predate the Bible entirely, show no evidence that such an event ever happened (appearance of the oldest book of the Hindu religion, the Rig Veda, pre-dates the Bible considerably, according to astronomical dating provided by astronomical events listed in the Rig Veda).

The Noah story is really telling us about our own God power of creation – a power of creation that we possess as an image of God.

The Bible is the division of the Hebrew Scriptures and, therefore, Hebrew and the Kabbalah are the point of origin to any research into this and other biblical stories, which are just that, metaphorical stories!

Noah, in Hebrew is two letters; 'Nun' which are the waters of creation and 'Chet' which is 'Life', therefore Noah is the life within the waters of creation (NUN-CHET).

It is the story of the child within its mother, whereby the child is protected by the mother's body (ark). It is known as arcane knowledge, or arcanum, which is knowledge only known by the informed.

The child develops in, what is known as, the 64 tetrahedron grid, and the 8 star tetrahedron makes up the 64 tetrahedron grid, hence why there were 8 people on Noah's ark. The aspect of the story of the animals going in 2 by 2 are the base pairs of DNA nucleotides, the foundation of life that exist in base pairs. It is a genetic/DNA reference. These nucleotides are adenine (A), thymine (T), guanine (G), and cytosine (C). A&T will always join together, and so will G&C. They exist as base pairs, two by two; this is the true meaning of the two by two referred to in the ark. Even some genealogists refer to them as the Noah's ark of chromosomes. We have 23 chromosomes from our father and 23 chromosomes from our mother.

The word for primordial waters of creation 'Nun' also gives us the religious Nuns who are pinnacle in Catholic circles, but from where does this originate?

Catholic means 'universal' and Vatican derives from 'Vatika' meaning the 'Third Eye'. In Egypt, the Primordial chaotic waters of creation (Primordial Mound) were called the 'Nun', referring to motherhood and fertility! The Goddess of motherhood and fertility is 'Isis', the 'superior Mother' (Mother Superior).

The word and Nunnery term 'Sister' derives from 'Isis-Star', which is 'Sirius A'' (associated with Isis).

Isis is also associated with the 'Moon', and Nuns live in a 'Monastery', deriving from 'Moon-aster', 'Moon-star'! The female body is locked into lunar cycles with menstruation, the 'Blood of Isis', the 'Tyet'.

(Tyet)

'Heaven' in Hebrew is 'Shamayim', the superior waters that fall from the sky and create the waters of Earth and within the body, namely the Mayim. When you see the Hebrew letters, you can see that 'Mayim' comes from within 'Shamayim'. The biblical dome/ firmament is the interaction between our world and the upper world, the two worlds.

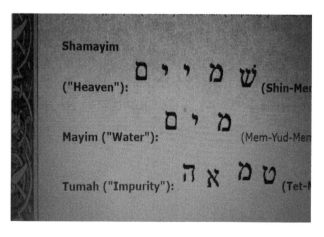

(Shamayim – Heaven & Mayim – Lower waters)

It is the MEM, the womb of Binah (understanding) where God resides as the Yud (gift) or Holy seed, and 'Holy' means 'Qodesh', which is to separate into a distinct element.

This Heaven (Shamayim) contains the womb of God and is referring to the divine womb, from which the newborn child enters a new world post-flood (mother's waters). We, too, have the God power to create life.

And it rained for 40 days and for 40 nights!

Again, the Mayim is represented by the number 40 and it is also relevant to the Judaic 'mikvah' bath, which is filled by natural water (rain) in volumes of 40 Se'ah. This bath is the recreation of the womb experience. A normal pregnancy is 40 weeks.

Noah and the ark is not a real boat or a real person. It is a metaphor for the creation of the child through the connection of the fishes of the creational waters, sperm, and the ovum, the combined forces of human creation.

This is really Noah and the Arcanum.

TWELVE

THE MYSTERY OF EASTER ISLAND

You approach Easter Island, a Chilean island in the Pacific Ocean, and you see what appears to be an abandoned gigantic game of chess on the surface of the landscape. Numerous large stone heads all look at you, and you look back in both wonderment and intrigue that still today poses many questions.

I have spent many years piecing together the ancient world and I have deciphered a hidden code that connects them all. When you are situated at the centre of a grid, it is much easier to piece together the whole grid itself, which is what I have done. The spider on the geometric fabric web can sense what is happening throughout his domain.

When you see the same numbers and the same message repeatedly, then it is safe to say that there is a bigger meaning to it, a bigger meaning as to why these numbers and this message is consistently used. It is a key, it is a hidden code.

Regardless of the monument, and regardless of the religious scripture, the message is the same across the whole of the ancient world. That message is one of 'Human Enlightenment and Human Consciousness'.

The heads of Easter Island are no different and hold onto a secret message of self. Here's how!

The heads of Easter Island all face east (Easter) and, in cardinal points, east represents illumination and enlightenment, the location of the rise of the Sun, which is also why the Sphinx of Egypt and Egyptian mummies face that direction. There are 1000 heads at Easter Island, and the number 1000 is the highest level of consciousness, as per the 1000 petaled lotus flower of Buddhism. 1000 also represents aleph (alef) which is one which has a value of 34, introspection and inner wisdom.

The heads themselves are energy emitters of 'Negative Green', which are radio waves and facilitators of communication with the higher realms - in effect, radio waves that carry information - and the word Moai, the name of the inhabitants of the island, means 'to listen'. The stones absorb Earth's energy waves and transmute them. And I have previously mentioned in another chapter the Herma which is the divine mind.

The statues are 33 feet high, which is highly significant as the frequency of our own Christ Consciousness is 33 hertz, hence why we are told, biblically, that Jesus died aged 33 in the year 33AD. It is a hidden reference to this frequency of raised inner consciousness.

When we see the full bodies of the statues, we can see that their hands point towards their naval chakra, which indicates 'Inner Transformation'.

A face is a mathematical message of the 'golden ratio', which is the geometric foundation of creation itself. It is bound by this numerology, which is our arrival on the scene as a race of beings.

The DNA molecule, the program for all life, is also based on the golden section.

It measures 34 angstroms long by 21 angstroms wide for each full cycle of its double helix spiral. 34 and 21, of course, are numbers in the Fibonacci series and their ratio, 1.6190476, closely approximates phi, 1.6180339. The numerical value of the word one is 34 which is 3+4=7. It is the introspection which is finding answers within. 34 is the knowledge of self. 7 is the triumph of spirit over matter.

We are, as humans, genetic royalty, and we are much more than simple flesh and blood finite beings. These ancient messages, left for us throughout the ancient world, are indicators of our own greatness and potential.

It matters not whether those monuments are stone circle monoliths, the many pyramids around the world (and beyond Earth), or gigantic stone heads, the message is the same. Only the shape of the monuments ever changed, not their meanings.

Our bodies, just like the monoliths, are receiver and transmitter antennas that connect the Earth to the sky.

The ancients understood that connection, a connection that has been lost by the modern era.

THIRTEEN

KING ARTHUR, SANTA CLAUS, AND THE PIRATES TREASURE MAP

KING ARTHUR

Childhood imagination is a wonderful memory, seemingly lost in adulthood when life becomes serious, with the many stories that once took our minds on a mental vacation. One such story, although believed by many to be true and that he will return one day, is the legend of King Arthur, and you may be unsurprised to know that this story too is a metaphor. It is a metaphor for consciousness.

The name 'Arthur' derives from 'artos', which means 'bear' in the Celtic language, and a bear is symbolic of introspection - the examination of one's own conscious thoughts and knowledge. 'Avalon' derives from the word 'Avaloch', meaning 'the place of apples', and I have already shown you in a previous chapter the apple and its relationship to the pentagram, the symbol of the mysteries.

The famous round table is equality and balance, which is required to reach a higher mind and a higher God-state consciousness or, as the Arthur story tells us, Lancelot, which means God-like.

In occult philosophy, the sword is also related to wisdom and reason by the issuance of your words with the tongue of your mouth. Quite simply, the sword is used for cutting at a foe. Just like a physical sword can kill or maim your opponents, your mouth can issue sharp words that act like a sword to slay ignorance, lies, and darkness in the world in order to bring light.

Arthur's sword is Excalibur, which derives from 'Ex-Calce-Liberatus', meaning 'liberated from the stone'. The stone is the foundation stone or the stone of wisdom, which is our pineal gland. So what is this telling us? Arthur, the chosen, was the only person able to remove the sword from the stone, in other words, only the initiates, those chosen to receive the sacred knowledge, can remove that knowledge from the pineal gland. The hand appearing out of the water symbolises the rebirth of self. Merlin is our own inner alchemy and wizardry that transmutes us by means of the philosopher's stone, the gold of enlightenment. Camelot, Arthur's castle, was said to have been built with the fire of the dragon, which is our inner Kundalini serpent, energy of raising consciousness which, when overcome, turns us into a dragon master. The surname of Arthur is Pendragon, which means 'dragon master'!

Even the Norse God, Odin, sacrificed one eye at the well in exchange for knowledge, and one eye is the single eye and the pineal gland. Odin or, in old Saxon, Woden which, in proto-Germanic, is Wooanaz, means 'master of ecstasy'. Ecstasy means a trance-like state, originally one involving an experience of mystic self-transcendence, namely enlightenment.

The theme is, yet again, one of enlightened consciousness.

SANTA CLAUS – THE HOLY CLAUSTRUM...

The imagination of children the world over is now focused upon one date, the 25th December, when they will be visited by Santa...

They've waited all year for this time, and the excitement can now be felt...

As adults we, of course, know that Santa Claus is a fictional person, but what is he really? Santa Claus is second only in fame to Jesus who, himself, was not a real person, as you have already seen.

As with the real messages of biblical characters, and as with ancient cultural enlightenment at the top of society's knowledge base, Santa is no different. He is an aspect of the human brain called the claustrum. The claustrum coordinates the input and output across the brain and creates consciousness...

So this is how the story really goes!

The Claustrum (Santa Claus) is located (lives) in the human head as part of the Cortex, which is at the very top of the body: our internal North Pole! The Claustrum is surrounded by White Matter (snow) in the brain. Directly next to it can be found the External and the Extreme Capsule, which resemble a sleigh... It is also lateral to the Putamen ("consideration" – latin 'putare': "to consider, to think"), which is symbolised by the red cap that is worn by Santa Claus... The Putamen is connected to the Substantia Nigra (latin: "black substance", coal), which is involved in the process of regulating reward and addictions, and appears dark because it contains high levels of Neuromelanin. A unique feature of the Claustrum is that there is a uniformity in the function of its cells. All Neurons do the same work, and these Neurons are Santa's Elves... His helpers...

The suture of the skull (suture = the process of joining two surfaces or edges together) is the external entry point (chimney) of the planetary Santa Claus, where he enters your head (roof top). The internal chimney is the human spine.

THE INNER MAP OF TREASURE

So there you have it, the story of Santa is really the inner workings of the brain.

If, like me, you grew up as a teenager in the 1980s with movies such as *The Goonies*, *Treasure Island*, and others, or even if you're from a more modern era with the likes of *Pirates of the Caribbean*, you will be aware of the thieves of the high seas, the Pirates.

The search for treasure marked on the famous treasure map, the finder of which would be guaranteed the accumulation of riches. The parrot on their shoulder, the eye patch covering one eye, and the wooden ship showing the flag of death, the skull and crossbones. The skull and crossbones are a symbol of death, or at least this is the most understood meaning of this symbol, but what if that death was the death of the 'Old Testament' that marked the birth of a 'New Testament'? And, by testament, I refer to its actual meaning of body and mind! So what if this whole creation of the pirate and their symbols was actually telling us something deeper, so deep, in fact, that we cannot see it because it is referring to the most neglected aspect of life, which is ourselves?

The skull and crossbones are also associated with secret societies and, by virtue of this fact, it has a hidden meaning.

I have, over the last several years but more concentrated over the past 12 months, delved deep into the world of the esoteric, particularly ancient cultures. I have found that they all portrayed a message, and that message was one of self-enlightenment, reached by the magic of their monuments which show us how they did it. It was an advanced knowledge that has stood the test of time.

So, with this in mind, I can see a clear connection in the whole pirate philosophy, and here's how:

For the religious people out there, especially Christians, their Christ was crucified in Golgotha, the place of skulls, and there's the first clue. The skull, or head, is where the Christ consciousness exists.

I have explained in my books that the Christ, or more to the point the Christ seed, is crucified on the cross, which is the Optic Chiasm (known as the crossing) inside the brain, where 'X' marks the spot and, of course, 'X' also marks the spot on a treasure map.

X also gives us the skull and crossbones, the symbol of Osiris in Egypt, and the pathway to Christ consciousness within the mind, which is the hidden meaning of this symbol. The covering of one is symbolic of either the eye of Horus or Isis (right eye is Horus, left eye is Isis) and the eye patch holds relevance to this.

Spiritually, in animal symbology, the parrot represents the immense power of our inner mind which, again, is connected to consciousness, thought being the prerequisite to manifestation and conscious connection to the higher realms.

So, what about the hidden treasure?

Treasure, most prominently, is gold and gold is connected to both enlightenment and the Sun which aids our enlightenment, but we need to find it, we need to dig and retrieve what is within and find the treasure or, in other words, the collection of wisdom held within our skull and its third eye system.

And when we read the *Treasure Island* story, we hear about the 'Black Spot'. The Black Spot is a literary device invented by Robert Louis Stevenson for his novel, *Treasure Island*. In the book, pirates are presented with a black spot. He was a member of the Philosophical Society, and philosophy is knowledge.

When we, again, go back to Ancient Egypt, they had a Black Dot called the 'Aten', which is their representation of the Bindi in Hinduism and it locates the pineal gland, a part of our inner consciousness, the third eye. This can be seen hidden within the modern car logo Mini. The wings have multiple meanings; they represent the culmination of alchemical practices and balance, and the hemispheres of the cerebellum which deals with equilibrium.

(Mini Logo)

So there's my take on the whole scenario of pirates; they are, of course, real, but when we look into the world of symbology, a different language is often being spoken.

That language is consciousness and knowledge.

FOURTEEN

CONCLUSION

It was George Bernard Shaw that once said *"all great truths begin as blasphemies"*, and many may accuse the religious aspects of this book of being blasphemous. But those claims are from an inadequate thought process. No intent was placed into this book to offend or deny the existence of any of the world's most famous characters and the world's most famous stories. But the book did intend to express that these characters and stories are different to that originally taught and that which is still being taught, in fact, they are much different! This book takes you to the heart of esoteric and mystical teachings. So all the most famous biblical characters are living within us all and the wondrous ancient monuments are also replicating and representing the unseen universe within us too. Isn't that a good indication of our true potential, and isn't that enough for those with sinister motives to want to keep that information away from us all? How unifying would it be in this world without the petty arguments over religions and Gods? What if we could all unite behind one creator and just admit to ourselves and to each other that we are all a part of the same race and that there is no need, or no place, for division or segregation?

The Bible and our ancient past is the same story told over and over again by different people who expressed that very same story in their own way but, nevertheless, they are all referring to the same hidden message and all are referring to the same meaning. That message is how to reach higher levels of self through elevated levels of self-awareness, and this is also what the ancient monuments are expressing to us. Great lengths have been taken to hide this secret from those who aren't receptive enough to receive. The names and locations have, in many cases, changed, but the secret wisdom hasn't. All religions are, in fact, the same bark of a large tree, but the branches of that tree are the public levels of faith and the branches are the diversion away from the bark, the bark being true Gnosis. It was always a passion of mine to know the truth; even from a very young age I was very much different in that respect. I observed rather than spoke, I listened rather than commented, and I pondered and contemplated rather than assumed belief. I questioned why, and I questioned everything from a quiet and secluded corner of every room. Why do people believe what they believe? Where does it come from and who is behind it? When I visited buildings of mystique, I knew that within its architecture was the answers, it contained a hidden language that only certain initiates could see. I soon began to read their script and I soon began to decipher their ancient language.

The esoteric truth hidden within, the key to enlightenment and success was pictorially concealed in glass and mortar. Celebrations of religious festivals meant something different to me than it did to the congregation and even the priests. I was the fish on land, the loner, and the thinking man. The world seemed backwards to me, nothing followed a logical order, schooling taught me false history, society tried to teach me to accept slavery, and governments tried to tell me that is was a good system.

The Bible was not written by God, it was written by man with the knowledge of what God is, man, whose intent was to hide how we re-connect to the creative force that is God. To believe is to 'be-leave', which is to be absent, and there are far too many absentees.

2019 years after the supposed death of Christ people still believe the same stories and not always through personal belief, many because of generations of programming from parents and society. If something is repeated often enough and is the only version allowed to be seen or heard then, eventually, it is accepted as truth, even when it isn't. If I only ever get shown red and everyone around tells me that red is the only colour, then I start to see red as the truth and the only truth. My viewpoint is limited to the extent that I cannot see the rainbow. It is a mark of advancement to see that other colours exist. Religion is divisive but, at its true origins, it could be unifying. Little do its followers realise, through their own ignorance, that they are actually worshipping the same Gods and the same icons and yet they cannot see it. They will all be waiting a long, long time for an external saviour, because there isn't one. People still believe that the pyramids of Egypt were a burial chamber and they believe much of what is told is true.

Salvation comes from within, and we all have the power to save ourselves. All of the ancient cultures of the world have been telling us this for many thousands of years. We are the only ones capable of such salvation, no-one else and nothing else can do it for us. When you realise this, your world opens up to a width, length, and depth that elevates you to a place of euphoria. What I am telling you is that you are Jesus Christ, that you are Mary Magdalene, that you are Moses and Noah and Jonah and Mary and Joseph and John the Baptist, etc. And this is because their stories are stories of all of us as human beings. None of them were real individuals or real people. Those at the helm of belief systems know this, and have always known this.

"It has served us well, this myth of Christ" – Pope Leo X

Do you not think that if people were told of their own greatness instead of being threatened with punishment, Hell, and damnation for not following a certain doctrine that it would be both liberating and unifying? Do people not think that a God who is vengeful, jealous, and murders people is a true God of love? How ridiculous. The Bible is littered with stories of God's genocide, and this is precisely how these things can be used to control people, because people have seemingly lost the ability to think for themselves. Any God who acts and behaves in the way the biblical God is portrayed is a man-made entity to control minds and lives. Someone once remarked to me at an event I had attended, *"So everyone was brought up on a lie, except you?"* I said, *"No, I was brought up on the same lie but I saw through it"*. Those with the eyes that can see and the ears that can hear will always do so.

The world is under the grip of secret and hidden codes, a language that not many speak ciphered into the fabric of society, in its buildings, literature, and its belief system.

Break the codes and you speak the language!

They use codes to hide the truth, and a code is a method of communication but much more intriguing is hidden code, because hidden code is deliberate concealment. We live in a world full of hidden codes and secret languages that are only spoken by and understood by the initiates of the brotherhoods and not the average man/women on the street who simply pass them by each and every day. And this is completely deliberate! When you speak the coded languages of these initiates, when you know what they know, the world of their language becomes your own native tongue! I have deciphered their codes, I speak their language, and I can tell you that our history is deliberately falsified. It is now time to start anew, we have the knowledge, and we have the means. So, in ancient philosophy, let us resurrect and ascend to our rightful levels.

It is the second law of thermodynamics that when energy changes from one form to another format, or matter moves freely, the entropy in a closed system increases. If over 50% of your brain believes that anything is possible, the strong thought will draw you by inductive resonance to the timeline where it is reality. Inductive resonance means magnetically pulled.

So believe in the law of attraction!

There has been an intervention that is giving us the tools to become a higher type of genetic human and a higher type of conscious human.

We are the Gods.

My kindest regards,

Michael

www.michael-feeley.com

Self-Publishing Your Book Made Easy!

Michael's Publisher Sazmick Books, offer self-publishing, editing and marketing services to authors of most genres. We help to fulfill your ambition of getting your work from typed or written manuscript, into a printed book or E-book with customisable add-ons. Simple packages, Stunning books. Chat with us and get your book on the road today!

www.sazmickbooks.com

For All Your Self-Publishing Needs

BV - #0034 - 291221 - C0 - 216/138/18 - PB - 9781912400058 - Gloss Lamination